CW00521599

Animal Fortune-telling

Charanavi

Explore your personality and improve your relationships

Masahiro Tsurumoto

Translated by **Chikako Saito**

NATURAL SPIRIT

Santa Monica, California

© 2007 Masahiro Tsurumoto
All rights reserved.

No portion of this book may be reproduced or used in any form, or by any means, without prior written permission of the publishers.

Translated by Chikako Saito
Illustrations by Shinji Nishikawa

Cover and interior design by Lightbourne, Inc.

Published by Natural Spirit International, Inc.
854 Pico Blvd.
Santa Monica, CA 90405
Phone: 310-581-1023
Fax: 310-581-1073
www.naturalspirit.us
info@naturalspirit.us

Printed in China by Palace Press International

First printed April 2007

10 9 8 7 6 5 4 3 2 1

Library of Congress Catalog Card Number: 2007922502

ISBN: 978-1-934140-00-0

Contents

Preface 4

How to Find Your Animal Character 8

How to Use the Charanavi System 14

Animal Characters:

Wolf 22

Fawn 36

Monkey 46

Cheetah 60

Black Panther 70

Lion 84

Tiger 94

Tanuki 108

Koala 118

Elephant 132

Sheep 142

Pegasus 156

Conversations 166

Business Settings 168

Party Scene 170

Male & Female Compatibility Chart 172

My Charanavi Companions 180

Character Index 183

The Author & Production Team 184

Preface

In 1997, "Koseishinrigaku" (or Personality Psychology/Character Navigation Psychology) was developed as the first theory to analyze personality types by pairing them with 12 unique animal characters.

It was soon featured on television and in many magazines—and the result was that my books became bestsellers. Charanavi (which stands for "character navigation") has been quite well-known throughout Japan since 2000, and now it is nearly common knowledge.

I take pleasure in knowing that Charanavi is widely recognized as a communication tool, rather than a psychology theory or fortune-telling system.

It has been introduced in college lectures and as a training course in major companies, as well as hospitals and schools. We often hear the names of these animal characters in daily conversation, and I can see that Charanavi has now become very familiar to many.

Recently, it has been gaining popularity in France, China, Korea, Taiwan, Thailand and other places globally through lectures and published materials. In 2003, Charanavi came to the United States, establishing a corporation in Las Vegas and publishing a magazine in Los Angeles and San Francisco. Since that time, Charanavi fans have been gradually increasing in the U.S.A. Certified Charanavi lecturers/instructors who are helping to introduce the theories of this communication tool are becoming popular as well.

Having this opportunity to publish the Charanavi book in English, I feel the utmost joy in offering this tool not only to the people of the U.S., but to English speakers all over the world. I would like to thank all of the people who have been so helpful in taking on this project.

Now, I will tell you a few details about myself—why I came to believe that I should establish the theory of Charanavi and share it with the world.

When I was four years old, I suffered a terrible fall over the edge of a cliff. I lost consciousness and was in critical condition. The doctors informed my family that there was no hope of recovery and that they should prepare for the worst.

While unconscious, I found myself walking in a land filled with a light I had never experienced before. It was a place that some might call "heaven." It was filled with brilliant light and wonderful fragrances, and I was in no pain at all. I felt love and gratitude as if they had arisen from deep within my soul.

But then I heard my parents calling me desperately, whole-heartedly, from far away.

I wanted to walk toward the brilliant light in the distance, but I could not help looking back upon hearing my parents' voices.

I stopped to think for a while, feeling a conflict inside. Soon, I heard a voice from the light, saying "Go back . . ."

After hearing this voice, I was brought back to consciousness. I felt intense pain and realized that I was back on earth. My parents and family were all very happy, but I could not forget what I had experienced while unconscious. I kept it to myself, believing that I should not share it with anyone.

Later, I had several near-death experiences and became fascinated with the afterlife. I began to research the concepts of reincarnation, the soul, life force and many other topics in spirituality, and my interests extended to the wonders of the universe, as well as history and world cultures.

There were so many questions: Why do we come into being? What's the difference between humans and other living beings? Where do we go after we die? The more I read and studied, the deeper I was taken with the mystery of our existence.

Since I had not previously shared what I have experienced in the world beyond, I sometimes have difficulty in explaining these things. But I would like to share with you my last experience in the afterlife—I received the marvelous answer to my question, "Why do I have to go back to earth?"

The answer was, "Because you have not fulfilled your mission yet."

The voice continued, "When human souls decide to come into the world, they choose their parents at their own will. They choose their surroundings, appearance and the entire situation throughout their lives. Before birth this is not a mystery, because every soul knows its mission. But at the moment of birth, the mission and memories of the life before this life on earth are forgotten. That is why people suffer. When a baby is born, no matter in what country, a name is given to him/her. This name stands for their mission. [In Japanese, the word for "mission" is homonymous with the word for "full name."] Throughout your life, you will be called by your name and will write it down hundreds and thousands of times so that you will not forget your mission . . ."

Yes. We have chosen our life for ourselves. In fact, our appearance, our character and personality, etc., are all what we have selected for our lifetime. But without knowing this, we often wonder "Why am I not beautiful?" or we think to ourselves "I wish I were born with a different personality," and we find it difficult to accept ourselves.

After I graduated from the university, I worked for one of the major insurance companies in Japan. I thought my work might allow me to take part in matters of "life and death." But to my regret, big companies only valued the calculated data concerning the rate of accidents and deaths. Things that we could not see were denied, and so it was quite different from what I had imagined.

So I decided to live my life according to my mission. As I have mentioned above, I established the Institute of Koseishinrigaku in 1997 and began to research the human personality using ancient Chinese statistical data.

The concept of utilizing animal characters to analyze personality types comes from the method of image psychology—which conveys that it has been proven that our memories only remain as images. I also understood that if the theories were complex, they may not be easily understood by the general public. So I aimed for an easy-to-understand psychology that can be loved by everyone, from children to adults. Perhaps this is why Charanavi has been warmly accepted by people all over the world, of all ages and occupations.

I hope you will recognize the unique differences between these Charanavi characters—and that in these differences is an inherent value through which we can create better communication with others. I truly wish that by reading and utilizing Charanavi, we all may help to create a more harmonious and less stressful world.

You can utilize Charanavi in various ways, such as in business environments, one-on-one relations, parenting and family settings, etc. I invite you all to please enjoy using this book.

Thank you, thank you, thank you!

With many blessings,

Masahiro Tsurumoto

(Glorious TANUKI*)

Director of the Institute of Koseishinrigaku

*TANUKI: *The tanuki is an indigenous animal of Japan, similar to a raccoon or badger. Well known throughout Japan not only as a wild animal but also as a cultural figure, the tanuki often appears in folktales. Often compared to the fox, the tanuki is known for taking on the shape of other creatures or objects. While the fox is famous for its cunning character, the tanuki is jolly and somewhat gullible. It is widely accepted as a lovable creature.*

Your Animal Character

4 simple steps to finding your number, character and group

(1)

EXAMPLE • **If your birthday is April 29, 1957:**

Look at **Table 1** and find the number where your birth-year line (1957) and birth-month line (April) cross. ➲ **39**

(2)

Add your birth-day (**29**) to this number, and the sum will be your character number.

➲ **39+29 = 68**

If the sum is over 60, subtract 60 from the sum number.

➲ **68–60 = 8**

Note 1: *If you were born in the southern hemisphere, add 30 to the sum number, and if the sum is over 60, subtract 60.*

Note 2: *If you are not sure about your birth time, or if you were born around midnight, be sure to calculate and read the characteristics for the days before and after (±1). Whichever character describes you best is your Charanavi animal.*

(3)

Look at **Table 2** and find the animal character numbered **8**.
➲ **Glorious TANUKI**

(4)

In **Table 2**, you will also see the illustrated moon, which shows that you are in the **Moon Group** for the **Moon**, **Earth**, **Sun** classification.

Your results are as follows:

- Out of the twelve animal types, your character grouping is **TANUKI**.

- From the 60 varieties, your detailed character is **Glorious TANUKI**.

- Within the Moon, Earth, Sun grouping, your type is **Moon**.

Find your character online today at www.charanaviusa.com

Table 1 · Charanavi Conversion Table (1908–1942)

Year/Month	Jan	Feb	Mar	Apr	May	Jun	Jul	Aug	Sep	Oct	Nov	Dec
1908	51	22	51	22	52	23	53	24	55	25	56	26
1909	57	28	56	27	57	28	58	29	0	30	1	31
1910	2	33	1	32	2	33	3	34	5	35	6	36
1911	7	38	6	37	7	38	8	39	10	40	11	41
1912	12	43	12	43	13	44	14	45	16	46	17	47
1913	18	49	17	48	18	49	19	50	21	51	22	52
1914	23	54	22	53	23	54	24	55	26	56	27	57
1915	28	59	27	58	28	59	29	0	31	1	32	2
1916	33	4	33	4	34	5	35	6	37	7	38	8
1917	39	10	38	9	39	10	40	11	42	12	43	13
1918	44	15	43	14	44	15	45	16	47	17	48	18
1919	49	20	48	19	49	20	50	21	52	22	53	23
1920	54	25	54	25	55	26	56	27	58	28	59	29
1921	0	31	59	30	0	31	1	32	3	33	4	34
1922	5	36	4	35	5	36	6	37	8	38	9	39
1923	10	41	9	40	10	41	11	42	13	43	14	44
1924	15	46	15	46	16	47	17	48	19	49	20	50
1925	21	52	20	51	21	52	22	53	24	54	25	55
1926	26	57	25	56	26	57	27	58	29	59	30	0
1927	31	2	30	1	31	2	32	3	34	4	35	5
1928	36	7	36	7	37	8	38	9	40	10	41	11
1929	42	13	41	12	42	13	43	14	45	15	46	16
1930	47	18	46	17	47	18	48	19	50	20	51	21
1931	52	23	51	22	52	23	53	24	55	25	56	26
1932	57	28	57	28	58	29	59	30	1	31	2	32
1933	3	34	2	33	3	34	4	35	6	36	7	37
1934	8	39	7	38	8	39	9	40	11	41	12	42
1935	13	44	12	43	13	44	14	45	16	46	17	47
1936	18	49	18	49	19	50	20	51	22	52	23	53
1937	24	55	23	54	24	55	25	56	27	57	28	58
1938	29	0	28	59	29	0	30	1	32	2	33	3
1939	34	5	33	4	34	5	35	6	37	7	38	8
1940	39	10	39	10	40	11	41	12	43	13	44	14
1941	45	16	44	15	45	16	46	17	48	18	49	19
1942	50	21	49	20	50	21	51	22	53	23	54	24

CONTINUED ON NEXT PAGE >

Table 1 · Charanavi Conversion Table (1943–1977)

Year/Month	Jan	Feb	Mar	Apr	May	Jun	Jul	Aug	Sep	Oct	Nov	Dec
1943	55	26	54	25	55	26	56	27	58	28	59	29
1944	0	31	0	31	1	32	2	33	4	34	5	35
1945	6	37	5	36	6	37	7	38	9	39	10	40
1946	11	42	10	41	11	42	12	43	14	44	15	45
1947	16	47	15	46	16	47	17	48	19	49	20	50
1948	21	52	21	52	22	53	23	54	25	55	26	56
1949	27	58	26	57	27	58	28	59	30	0	31	1
1950	32	3	31	2	32	3	33	4	35	5	36	6
1951	37	8	36	7	37	8	38	9	40	10	41	11
1952	42	13	42	13	43	14	44	15	46	16	47	17
1953	48	19	47	18	48	19	49	20	51	21	52	22
1954	53	24	52	23	53	24	54	25	56	26	57	27
1955	58	29	57	28	58	29	59	30	1	31	2	32
1956	3	34	3	34	4	35	5	36	7	37	8	38
1957	9	40	8	39	9	40	10	41	12	42	13	43
1958	14	45	13	44	14	45	15	46	17	47	18	48
1959	19	50	18	49	19	50	20	51	22	52	23	53
1960	24	55	24	55	25	56	26	57	28	58	29	59
1961	30	1	29	0	30	1	31	2	33	3	34	4
1962	35	6	34	5	35	6	36	7	38	8	39	9
1963	40	11	39	10	40	11	41	12	43	13	44	14
1964	45	16	45	16	46	17	47	18	49	19	50	20
1965	51	22	50	21	51	22	52	23	54	24	55	25
1966	56	27	55	26	56	27	57	28	59	29	0	30
1967	1	32	0	31	1	32	2	33	4	34	5	35
1968	6	37	6	37	7	38	8	39	10	40	11	41
1969	12	43	11	42	12	43	13	44	15	45	16	46
1970	17	48	16	47	17	48	18	49	20	50	21	51
1971	22	53	21	52	22	53	23	54	25	55	26	56
1972	27	58	27	58	28	59	29	0	31	1	32	2
1973	33	4	32	3	33	4	34	5	36	6	37	7
1974	38	9	37	8	38	9	39	10	41	11	42	12
1975	43	14	42	13	43	14	44	15	46	16	47	17
1976	48	19	48	19	49	20	50	21	52	22	53	23
1977	54	25	53	24	54	25	55	26	57	27	58	28

CONTINUED ON NEXT PAGE >

Table 1 · Charanavi Conversion Table (1978–2012)

Year/Month	Jan	Feb	Mar	Apr	May	Jun	Jul	Aug	Sep	Oct	Nov	Dec
1978	59	30	58	29	59	30	0	31	2	32	3	33
1979	4	35	3	34	4	35	5	36	7	37	8	38
1980	9	40	9	40	10	41	11	42	13	43	14	44
1981	15	46	14	45	15	46	16	47	18	48	19	49
1982	20	51	19	50	20	51	21	52	23	53	24	54
1983	25	56	24	55	25	56	26	57	28	58	29	59
1984	30	1	30	1	31	2	32	3	34	4	35	5
1985	36	7	35	6	36	7	37	8	39	9	40	10
1986	41	12	40	11	41	12	42	13	44	14	45	15
1987	46	17	45	16	46	17	47	18	49	19	50	20
1988	51	22	51	22	52	23	53	24	55	25	56	26
1989	57	28	56	27	57	28	58	29	0	30	1	31
1990	2	33	1	32	2	33	3	34	5	35	6	36
1991	7	38	6	37	7	38	8	39	10	40	11	41
1992	12	43	12	43	13	44	14	45	16	46	17	47
1993	18	49	17	48	18	49	19	50	21	51	22	52
1994	23	54	22	53	23	54	24	55	26	56	27	57
1995	28	59	27	58	28	59	29	0	31	1	32	2
1996	33	4	33	4	34	5	35	6	37	7	38	8
1997	39	10	38	9	39	10	40	11	42	12	43	13
1998	44	15	43	14	44	15	45	16	47	17	48	18
1999	49	20	48	19	49	20	50	21	52	22	53	23
2000	54	25	54	25	55	26	56	27	58	28	59	29
2001	0	31	59	30	0	31	1	32	3	33	4	34
2002	5	36	4	35	5	36	6	37	8	38	9	39
2003	10	41	9	40	10	41	11	42	13	43	14	44
2004	15	46	15	46	16	47	17	48	19	49	20	50
2005	21	52	20	51	21	52	22	53	24	54	25	55
2006	26	57	25	56	26	57	27	58	29	59	30	60
2007	31	2	30	1	31	2	32	3	34	4	35	5
2008	36	7	36	7	37	8	38	9	40	10	41	11
2009	42	13	41	12	42	13	43	14	45	15	46	16
2010	47	18	46	17	47	18	48	19	50	20	51	21
2011	52	23	51	22	52	23	53	24	55	25	56	26
2012	57	28	57	28	58	29	59	30	1	31	2	32

Table 2 · 60 Animal Characters

Number	Character Name	Group	Page
1	Marathon CHEETAH	☀	62
2	Sociable TANUKI	☾	110
3	Restless MONKEY	☻	48
4	Swift KOALA	☻	120
5	Caring BLACK PANTHER	◑	72
6	Affectionate TIGER	☻	96
7	Sprinting CHEETAH	☀	64
8	Glorious TANUKI	☾	112
9	Ambitious MONKEY	☻	50
10	Merciful KOALA	☻	122
11	Honest FAWN	☾	38
12	Popular ELEPHANT	☀	134
13	Cheerful WOLF	☻	24
14	Solitary SHEEP	◯	144
15	Dignified MONKEY	☻	52
16	King KOALA	☻	124
17	Strong-Willed FAWN	☾	40
18	Delicate ELEPHANT	☀	136
19	Wandering WOLF	☻	26
20	Harmonious SHEEP	◯	146
21	Calm PEGASUS	☀	158
22	Flexible PEGASUS	☀	160
23	Innocent SHEEP	◯	148
24	Creative WOLF	☻	28
25	Gentle WOLF	☻	30
26	Humane SHEEP	◯	150
27	Dramatic PEGASUS	☀	162
28	Elegant PEGASUS	☀	164
29	Adventurous SHEEP	◯	152
30	Adaptable WOLF	☻	32

Table 2 · 60 Animal Characters continued

Number	Character Name	Group	Page
31	Chief ELEPHANT	☀	138
32	Steady FAWN	☾	42
33	Active KOALA	◑	126
34	Playful MONKEY	◑	54
35	Reliable SHEEP	○	154
36	Lovable WOLF	◑	34
37	Rushing ELEPHANT	☀	140
38	Beautiful FAWN	☾	44
39	Romantic KOALA	◑	128
40	Devoted MONKEY	◑	56
41	Potential TANUKI	☾	114
42	Tough CHEETAH	☀	66
43	Energetic TIGER	◑	98
44	Passionate BLACK PANTHER	○	74
45	Helpful KOALA	◑	130
46	Protective MONKEY	◑	58
47	Mighty-Hearted TANUKI	☾	116
48	Graceful CHEETAH	☀	68
49	Confident TIGER	◑	100
50	Sentimental BLACK PANTHER	○	76
51	Independent LION	☀	86
52	Captain LION	☀	88
53	Soulful BLACK PANTHER	○	78
54	Optimistic TIGER	◑	102
55	Powerful TIGER	◑	104
56	Friendly BLACK PANTHER	○	80
57	Emotional LION	☀	90
58	Sensitive LION	☀	92
59	Freedom-Loving BLACK PANTHER	○	82
60	Liberty TIGER	◑	106

How to Use the
Charanavi System

Moon, Earth and Sun Groups

The Law of Janken (rock-paper-scissors) is one of the basic theories of Charanavi.

Twelve animal characters are classified into three different groups: **Moon**, **Earth** and **Sun**. Members within each group easily understand one another. The three groups relate to each other in a "rock-paper-scissors" way, in which:

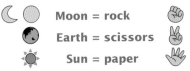

And they relate this way (win > lose), following the basic rock-paper-scissors rules: **Moon (rock) > Earth (scissors) > Sun (paper) > Moon (rock)**.

Communication and relationships are smoother this way (clockwise). But if reversed, it tends to be stressful. For example, if someone in the Earth group (e.g., wolf/scissors) is in a position of power over someone in the Sun group (e.g., elephant/paper), the relationship and communication go well because scissors beat paper according to the rock-paper-scissors rules. But if these positions are reversed, relationships tend to be stressful. A "position of power" in this context could mean a higher position at work or school (i.e., a superior or a professor), or in terms of age differences, it could be an elder or a parent.

Of course, this does not mean that the Earth group is greater than the Sun group. It is just the fascinating complexity of human relations that illustrates how different personality types communicate with one another. Remember that the person in the subordinate position tends to feel stress even though the person in the upper position might feel comfortable in the relationship. If you recognize this and accept your characteristics as well as others', your stress level will be reduced, and you can better understand how to get along with the person you are having difficulty with.

Moon group* (rock) = unity, persistence, close relationships

- don't like to fight or quarrel
- want to be humane
- aim to be an upright person with a noble character
- cherish warm relationships with others
- always consider the big picture
- have a questioning personality and often ask "Why?" and "What for?"
- weak in sorting out messes and disposing of things; tend to be wasteful

Moon group is further classified into two groups: New Moon and Full Moon.

New Moon (FAWN, TANUKI)

Even if you are not in a prominent position now, you will be happy to be in the limelight later on. Since you tend to be inconspicuous, you have a desire to be cared for or paid attention to. You are waiting for your time to "go on stage," and you are happy to be called.

Full Moon (BLACK PANTHER, SHEEP)

Since you have a fear of waning (i.e., fading out), you do not like to be ignored and tend to worry about your status, standpoint and position. You don't want to be forgotten and hate to be left out.

Earth group (scissors) = creating shape, cutting off useless things

- don't want interruption in your pace
- like to be in your own world
- aim to be a wealthy person
- need plans to make your dreams come true
- good at giving shape or expression to abstract concepts
- have a persistent personality and often say "I'll do my best" and "I'm convinced."
- tend to work too hard

Sun group (paper) = unfolding, expansion, explosion of energy

- hate restraints
- always wish to be active and bright
- aim to be a successful person
- need to turn a possibility into reality right away
- value the possibilities
- have an extroverted personality and often say "Great!" "Absolutely!" or "No way. It's too complicated."
- have ups and downs and tend to be moody

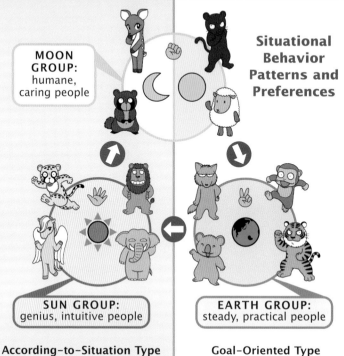

Situational Behavior Patterns and Preferences

MOON GROUP: humane, caring people

SUN GROUP: genius, intuitive people

EARTH GROUP: steady, practical people

According-to-Situation Type

- Need only a general outline of the plan and can proceed according to circumstances.

- Don't feel much stress even when things are not proceeding on schedule.

- Feel stress when a time limit is tightly fixed.

- Value good human relations and reveal your true intentions later.

- Strong in unexpected situations or with sudden changes and can show yourself at your best.

Goal-Oriented Type

- Need to have a clear purpose and want to carry out a plan as scheduled.

- Have clear distinctions between public and private life.

- Highly motivated when faced with a deadline but cannot be motivated if the deadline is not fixed.

- Believe that good human relations are rooted in speaking true intentions.

- Show difficulty in coping with shifting circumstances; weak in unexpected situations.

THINKING PATTERNS

Future-Prospect Type

- An optimist with a positive mind.
- Don't concern yourself with the past.
- While traveling, you pack lightly and buy whenever/wherever you need to.
- Motivation takes a hit when someone interferes after you've made up your mind.

Recollection Type

- Hate taking risks and proceed with utmost caution.
- Value experiences and achievements of the past.
- While traveling, you carry many things with you to feel secure.
- Motivation suffers when you are pressured into doing something.

THINKING STYLES

Right-Brain Type

- Have high spiritual energy.
- Fully utilize your imaginary powers and are very perceptive.
- Understand ideas and concepts best when explained with images rather than logic.

Left-Brain Type

- Have strong economic sensibilities.
- Face up to reality and regard data as important.
- Understand ideas and concepts best when explained with logic rather than images.

Character Relationships Chart

This chart illustrates how easy it is for a character to communicate with others. It shows the group each character belongs to (**moon**, **earth** or **sun**) and whether the character is **rock**, **paper** or **scissors**. In the Wolf's case, Elephants are very easy to communicate with, since the Wolf is scissors and the Elephant is paper (scissors beat paper). Wolf loses to Black Panther, Fawn and Tanuki (rock beats scissors), so relations with them can be stressful.

Use this chart to be aware of these communication tendencies, and remember that no matter what the percentage may be, we can always try to create better relations. Learn what each character likes and doesn't like. Use your imagination and acquaint yourself with each animal. *Enjoy the differences!*

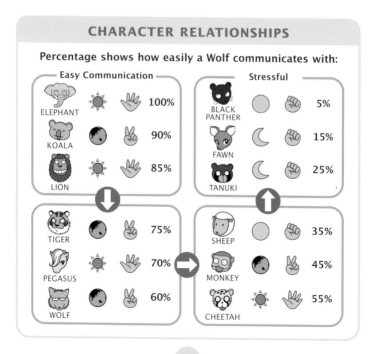

CHARACTER RELATIONSHIPS

Percentage shows how easily a Wolf communicates with:

Easy Communication

ELEPHANT			100%
KOALA			90%
LION			85%
TIGER			75%
PEGASUS			70%
WOLF			60%

Stressful

BLACK PANTHER			5%
FAWN			15%
TANUKI			25%
SHEEP			35%
MONKEY			45%
CHEETAH			55%

Success & Luck: Your Rhythm of Fortune

Know the best time to plan for finance, career, love *and more!*

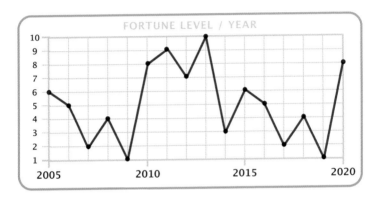

FORTUNE LEVEL / YEAR

This line graph shows **your fortune level** during each year from 2005 to 2020. Without knowing your life rhythm, you could miss a great opportunity to succeed when at a **high fortune level**, or you might start a new business (or expand) while at a **low fortune level**, which is not the right time to take action. With this line graph, you can know your fortune level and take the chance of a lifetime—and also prepare to overcome your low fortune period. Utilize this not only for your business career but also for your personal life.

10 point = Perfection: You will be successful in everything

This is the best period of your life. You will be very popular with the opposite sex. It is also a good time to consider marriage.

9 point = Success: Your best time for finance and competition

During this time, you can enjoy financial success and achievements in competition, sports and games.

8 point = Investment: A good time for networking and money

Your connections and network will expand, which might change your life. Live with a volunteering spirit, and utilize your money for investments.

7 point = Change: Start something new

This is a good time to make changes in your life, including career, home and love.

6 point = Learning: A time for studies and test-taking

Learn, study and take exams during this time. Particularly for women, it is a good time to consider marriage.

5 point = Action: Make your move while in good health

This is a good time to take positive action. You will be in good health.

4 point = Balance: Organize for harmony

Take the time to give your life a "tune-up." Organize and adjust your surroundings (pay attention to the people around you and your circumstances).

3 point = Arrangement: Clean up the clutter in your life

This is a good time to look at your relationships and personal matters to clean up the clutter in your life.

2 point = Waste: Watch your health and expenses

Pay attention to and take good care of your health during this time. Your expenses will tend to run high. Be conservative with your actions and energy.

1 point = Caution: Communicate carefully while preoccupied

During this time, be careful in your communication with others. While your mind is occupied with your own affairs and thoughts, you can tend to be impatient and irritated.

WOLF

- like to have your own time and space

- want to work at your own pace and hate for it to be disturbed

- do not like to copy others' styles

- a person of few words

- want to be recognized as a unique person

- give an unapproachable impression

- weak at responding to unexpected situations

. . . .

13 **Cheerful** Wolf

19 **Wandering** Wolf

24 **Creative** Wolf

25 **Gentle** Wolf

30 **Adaptable** Wolf

36 **Lovable** Wolf

CHARACTER RELATIONSHIPS

Percentage shows how easily a Wolf communicates with:

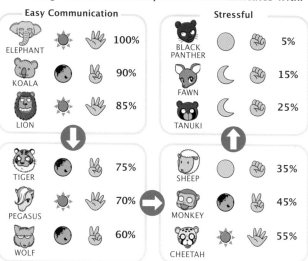

Easy Communication

ELEPHANT			100%
KOALA			90%
LION			85%

TIGER			75%
PEGASUS			70%
WOLF			60%

Stressful

BLACK PANTHER			5%
FAWN			15%
TANUKI			25%

SHEEP			35%
MONKEY			45%
CHEETAH			55%

TIPS & TABOOS: Understanding a Wolf

Words & phrases	Utilize words such as "unique," "original" and "rare" when praising them.
Places for a date	Places known to few people. They don't enjoy crowded or popular places.
Great gift ideas	Something rare. They enjoy receiving watches and prefer metallic textures.
Communication	Discuss how they differ from others. They like to talk about their uniqueness and originality.
Caution: Taboos	Never search for too much information. Saying "You are the same as others" is the worst taboo.

23

13 Cheerful WOLF

You look unapproachable and have a cool, businesslike appearance. In fact, you are somewhat indifferent to others. But after being a close friend of yours, people will understand that you have a pure heart. Since you rely on your own sense and keen intuition to see the world, what you say sometimes astonishes your friends. By utilizing this strength and making the most of your original ideas, you can set out on your own path to success. Since you are cheerful by nature and have a strong desire for justice, you will gradually gain a good reputation and popularity. Since you are not so susceptible to the influence of others, you can manage your life well and maintain your own individual lifestyle.

SUCCESS & LUCK: Your Rhythm of Fortune

Know the best time to plan for finance, career, love and more.

⑩ Perfection: You will be successful in everything

⑨ Success: Your best time for finance and competition

⑧ Investment: A good time for networking and money

⑦ Change: The right time to start something new

⑥ Learning: A time for studies and test-taking

⑤ Action: Make your move while in good health

④ Balance: Organize for harmony

③ Arrangement: Clean up the clutter in your life

② Waste: You tend to waste your time, energy and money

① Caution: Be careful in every way, especially when you are communicating with others

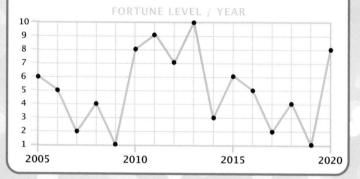

FORTUNE LEVEL / YEAR

♂ Has unique sensibilities and craftsmanship

♀ An individualist who prefers independent human relations

Famous Cheerful Wolves:

William Shatner. 3/22/1931
Calvin Klein. 11/19/1942
Jessica Alba. 4/28/1981

25

19 Wandering WOLF

You are a person with a unique viewpoint and can discover new ways of doing things without restraints of tradition or common sense. You are a challenger who always seeks change, but this does not mean that you are capricious. Having great ideas and the power to put things into practice, all you need is patience. Since you hate being irresponsible and always try to improve conditions, you will fulfill your dreams with strong will and vitality. You will not get into troublesome situations because you are protected by good fortune. Although you don't like to be emotionally intimate with others, you are such an honest and warmhearted person that you cannot say no to those who depend on you for help. Because of your unique personality, you are sometimes taken as an eccentric person, but you really cherish the love and relationship you have with the one who understands you best.

SUCCESS & LUCK: Your Rhythm of Fortune

Know the best time to plan for finance, career, love and more.

⑩ Perfection: You will be successful in everything

⑨ Success: Your best time for finance and competition

⑧ Investment: A good time for networking and money

⑦ Change: The right time to start something new

⑥ Learning: A time for studies and test-taking

⑤ Action: Make your move while in good health

④ Balance: Organize for harmony

③ Arrangement: Clean up the clutter in your life

② Waste: You tend to waste your time, energy and money

① Caution: Be careful in every way, especially when you are communicating with others

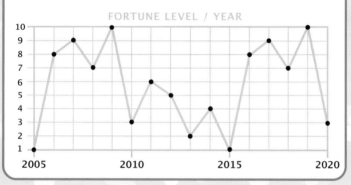

FORTUNE LEVEL / YEAR

♂ An adventurer who loves new things

♀ A traveler going her own way without the restraints of common sense

Famous Wandering Wolves:

John Glenn 7/18/1921
Jane Fonda 12/21/1937
Scottie Pippen 9/25/1965

27

24 Creative WOLF

You are a person with much knowledge and sophistication. Strong in science, mathematics and technology, you have the power to make steady efforts to gather data for continuous research and to come to a great conclusion. Since you do not care much about reputations, you make plans and carry them out at your own pace. Being friendly and frank, you are loved by others. But you harbor your own thoughts, so you don't necessarily depend on others. With a volunteering spirit, you work for others rather than for your own sake. You tend to value logic above all and might be taken as a stubborn person. While you see the world objectively without being emotional, you have a pure heart and can show your character well.

SUCCESS & LUCK: Your Rhythm of Fortune

Know the best time to plan for finance, career, love and more.

⑩ Perfection: You will be successful in everything

⑨ Success: Your best time for finance and competition

⑧ Investment: A good time for networking and money

⑦ Change: The right time to start something new

⑥ Learning: A time for studies and test-taking

⑤ Action: Make your move while in good health

④ Balance: Organize for harmony

③ Arrangement: Clean up the clutter in your life

② Waste: You tend to waste your time, energy and money

① Caution: Be careful in every way, especially when you are communicating with others

FORTUNE LEVEL / YEAR

 Scholarly and doesn't like to be under anyone's thumb

 Well-balanced, with a pure and calm heart

Famous Creative Wolves:

Hans Christian Andersen 4/2/1805
Akira Kurosawa 3/23/1910
Geena Davis 1/21/1956

25 Gentle WOLF

Although cheerful and friendly, you have an unapproachable atmosphere, and your superiority is often accepted. Since you are an honest, businesslike person with a sense of justice, you tend to say things too honestly. If you are a female, you might be taken as a blunt or indelicate person because you don't use flattery. But this frankness is your real charm. Since you are not sentimental and do not worry, you are cool-headed and very good at multitasking. You are a practical optimist who maintains your own unique lifestyle. Without being held back by the past or dreaming unreachable dreams, you are the type who will succeed in your later years. The older you get, the more respect you will gain.

SUCCESS & LUCK: Your Rhythm of Fortune

Know the best time to plan for finance, career, love and more.

⑩ Perfection: You will be successful in everything

⑨ Success: Your best time for finance and competition

⑧ Investment: A good time for networking and money

⑦ Change: The right time to start something new

⑥ Learning: A time for studies and test-taking

⑤ Action: Make your move while in good health

④ Balance: Organize for harmony

③ Arrangement: Clean up the clutter in your life

② Waste: You tend to waste your time, energy and money

① Caution: Be careful in every way, especially when you are communicating with others

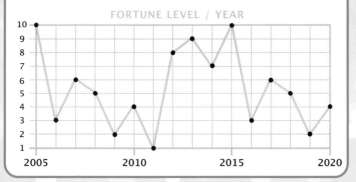

FORTUNE LEVEL / YEAR

♂ Has a childlike innocence and a noble spirit

♀ Realistic, with a girlish innocence

Famous Gentle Wolves:

Anne Frank 6/12/1929
Angie Dickinson 9/30/1931
David McCallum 9/19/1933

You are a rather aggressive person with a dignified manner. Since your communication is based on impartiality, you can give your honest, frank opinion even to your superiors. Calm and candid, you don't flatter, take advantage of others or turn against people. As your attitude and fashion reveal your intelligence, sometimes you give a formal and genteel impression. You do not sugarcoat your manner and have firm confidence in yourself, so you might be mistaken as a stubborn person. But as people get to know your true character, you will be respected and successful. You can make the most of your experiences in the future and steadily make your dreams come true by balancing with reality.

SUCCESS & LUCK: Your Rhythm of Fortune

Know the best time to plan for finance, career, love and more.

⑩ Perfection: You will be successful in everything

⑨ Success: Your best time for finance and competition

⑧ Investment: A good time for networking and money

⑦ Change: The right time to start something new

⑥ Learning: A time for studies and test-taking

⑤ Action: Make your move while in good health

④ Balance: Organize for harmony

③ Arrangement: Clean up the clutter in your life

② Waste: You tend to waste your time, energy and money

① Caution: Be careful in every way, especially when you are communicating with others

FORTUNE LEVEL / YEAR

♂ Powerful, dignified and can make dreams come true

♀ Calm and composed, with a fair and merciful nature

Famous Adaptable Wolves:

Benjamin Franklin 1/17/1706
Jackie Chan 4/7/1954
Cameron Diaz 8/30/1972

Y ou embody a "living common sense," always calm and objective. But since you are clever and multi-talented, and have a strong character, your impression is rather mysterious. Although you arouse others' attention, you are not easily understood. Your opinion is not biased or subjected to interests. But you are so sensitive that you are weak on communicating with others. It will take time, but if you live up to your principles and make the most of your character, you will call forth a surprising power. If you are a male, you may be taken as a cold-hearted person because you do not show your inner passion. You will be trusted for your reliable work, and since you are rational and objective, you will lead a full, fulfilling life without exertion.

SUCCESS & LUCK: Your Rhythm of Fortune

Know the best time to plan for finance, career, love and more.

10 Perfection: You will be successful in everything

9 Success: Your best time for finance and competition

8 Investment: A good time for networking and money

7 Change: The right time to start something new

6 Learning: A time for studies and test-taking

5 Action: Make your move while in good health

4 Balance: Organize for harmony

3 Arrangement: Clean up the clutter in your life

2 Waste: You tend to waste your time, energy and money

1 Caution: Be careful in every way, especially when you are communicating with others

FORTUNE LEVEL / YEAR

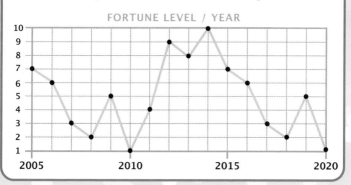

♂ Calm and gentle, with a mature air

♀ A talented and intelligent artist with a rich sense of humor

Famous Lovable Wolves:

Agatha Christie. 9/15/1890

Jet Li. 4/26/1963

Drew Barrymore. 2/22/1975

FAWN

- have strong likes and dislikes
- cannot tell a lie
- always want to feel loved
- like to be taken care of

- cannot hide your feelings
- full of curiosity
- good at educating people (training and teaching)

. . . .

11 **Honest** Fawn

17 **Strong-Willed** Fawn

32 **Steady** Fawn

38 **Beautiful** Fawn

CHARACTER RELATIONSHIPS

Percentage shows how easily a Fawn communicates with:

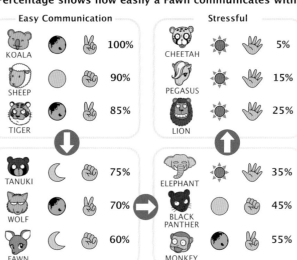

Easy Communication		Stressful	
KOALA	100%	CHEETAH	5%
SHEEP	90%	PEGASUS	15%
TIGER	85%	LION	25%
TANUKI	75%	ELEPHANT	35%
WOLF	70%	BLACK PANTHER	45%
FAWN	60%	MONKEY	55%

TIPS & TABOOS: Understanding a Fawn

Words & phrases	Use more flowery words such as "cute" and "lovely" liberally. Compliment their personal belongings (e.g., purse, wallet, watch).
Places for a date	Places with a fairytale or fantasy atmosphere (e.g., the aquarium or an art gallery with a nice view).
Great gift ideas	Little things such as mobile phone straps and cute trinkets.
Communication	Talk about friends and indulge them in rambling, endless conversations.
Caution: Taboos	They get angry when unable to get in touch with you frequently. It's not good to make jokes in the middle of conversation.

You have a simple, honest character with a natural manner, and you do not care much about your appearance. You are very cautious when meeting people for the first time, so you give the impression of having a gentle and quiet character. But as people get to know you better, your "sweet selfishness" comes out. You are not the type who is everybody's friend, but you have a few whom you can really trust throughout your life. Since you have strong likes and dislikes and hate injustice or wrong, you tend to be strict with others. Be careful not to be self-righteous. Your inner passion will lead you to your hopes and dreams, so you will always be young at heart. But since you do not have strong perseverance, you often abandon something or pass your success to others easily. This generosity is your charm, but remember not to give away what you possess so easily.

SUCCESS & LUCK: Your Rhythm of Fortune

Know the best time to plan for finance, career, love and more.

🔟 **Perfection**: You will be successful in everything

9️⃣ **Success**: Your best time for finance and competition

8️⃣ **Investment**: A good time for networking and money

7️⃣ **Change**: The right time to start something new

6️⃣ **Learning**: A time for studies and test-taking

5️⃣ **Action**: Make your move while in good health

4️⃣ **Balance**: Organize for harmony

3️⃣ **Arrangement**: Clean up the clutter in your life

2️⃣ **Waste**: You tend to waste your time, energy and money

1️⃣ **Caution**: Be careful in every way, especially when you are communicating with others

FORTUNE LEVEL / YEAR

♂ Passionate, with a young and pure heart

♀ Bright, charming and mischievous

Famous Honest Fawns:

Jacqueline Kennedy Onassis . . 7/28/1929
Bruce Lee 11/27/1940
Lisa Kudrow 7/30/1963

You appear intelligent and quiet and have a kind, gentle character. Although full of curiosity, you do not like big changes or upheaval in your daily life; you prefer to maintain present conditions and live within your means. You value seniority and politeness, hate quarreling, care much about your evaluations and are sensitive to rumors. You do not promote yourself, nor do you wish to be prominent. But you are rather competitive and self-confident at your core, and you have a fighting spirit and strong will. Since you have a sense of responsibility and dare to take risks when the time comes, you are much relied upon by others. Having the fortune to connect your interests to your line of business, you may be a leader in your field. You may also become a scholar or an artist.

SUCCESS & LUCK: Your Rhythm of Fortune

Know the best time to plan for finance, career, love and more.

10 Perfection: You will be successful in everything

9 Success: Your best time for finance and competition

8 Investment: A good time for networking and money

7 Change: The right time to start something new

6 Learning: A time for studies and test-taking

5 Action: Make your move while in good health

4 Balance: Organize for harmony

3 Arrangement: Clean up the clutter in your life

2 Waste: You tend to waste your time, energy and money

1 Caution: Be careful in every way, especially when you are communicating with others

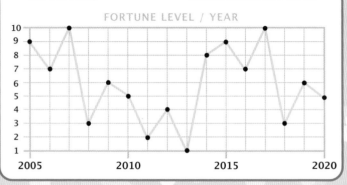

FORTUNE LEVEL / YEAR

 Strong-willed and never changes his standards

 Strives to save the weak

Famous Strong-Willed Fawns:

Giuseppe Verdi 10/10/1813
Dean Martin 6/7/1917
Hilary Duff 9/28/1987

You are a warmhearted person who always considers the feelings of others and ensures things work out so that no one gets hurt (including yourself). You love to please others, and being good-natured, you cannot say no to someone who asks for your help. Since you are gentle, you are valued for your ability to soften a situation. But on the contrary, you have a hasty side and can also handle things in a businesslike way. Inwardly, you play in a world of fantasy. Although you are somewhat capricious and selfish, you are so sweet that you will not be disliked by others. Since you are skilled at warding off the anger and bad tempers of those around you, you will not be bothered with much stress. You are the type who can lead a fulfilling life, given your gentle and unique social skills.

SUCCESS & LUCK: Your Rhythm of Fortune

Know the best time to plan for finance, career, love and more.

⑩ Perfection: You will be successful in everything

⑨ Success: Your best time for finance and competition

⑧ Investment: A good time for networking and money

⑦ Change: The right time to start something new

⑥ Learning: A time for studies and test-taking

⑤ Action: Make your move while in good health

④ Balance: Organize for harmony

③ Arrangement: Clean up the clutter in your life

② Waste: You tend to waste your time, energy and money

① Caution: Be careful in every way, especially when you are communicating with others

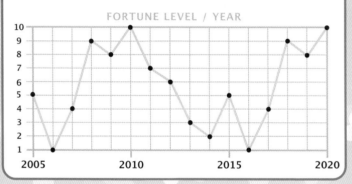

FORTUNE LEVEL / YEAR

A champion of justice who hates unreasonable situations

Sweet, childlike and loved by everyone

Famous Steady Fawns:

Peter Sellers 9/8/1925

Princess Diana 7/1/1961

Brad Pitt 12/18/1963

43

Since you truly hope to be loved by others, you seem very gentle and sociable. But you also have a somewhat mysterious air because you don't open your heart easily. Moreover, you are as pure as an innocent child, so your heart is often disturbed. You have strong likes and dislikes, and once you have decided that you hate something or someone, that means it is final. You tend to withdraw into your own world, and since you have no adherence to or interest in social success, you might not make the most of your opportunities. Your originality can help you cultivate a special sense of beauty, and your unexpected talent can blossom if you expand your interests to academic or artistic fields.

SUCCESS & LUCK: Your Rhythm of Fortune

Know the best time to plan for finance, career, love and more.

⑩ Perfection: You will be successful in everything

⑨ Success: Your best time for finance and competition

⑧ Investment: A good time for networking and money

⑦ Change: The right time to start something new

⑥ Learning: A time for studies and test-taking

⑤ Action: Make your move while in good health

④ Balance: Organize for harmony

③ Arrangement: Clean up the clutter in your life

② Waste: You tend to waste your time, energy and money

① Caution: Be careful in every way, especially when you are communicating with others

FORTUNE LEVEL / YEAR

○ Moody, with a strong sense of pride in himself

♀ A girlish dreamer with rich emotions

Famous Beautiful Fawns:

Joan of Arc 1/6/1412
Yo-Yo Ma 10/7/1955
Naomi Watts 9/28/1968

MONKEY

- tend to be restless

- skillful with your hands

- don't prefer a formal atmosphere

- work hard to be praised or rewarded

- need clear and definite instruction for tasks

- very competitive

- quick in decision and action

- -

3 **Restless** Monkey

9 **Ambitious** Monkey

15 **Dignified** Monkey

34 **Playful** Monkey

40 **Devoted** Monkey

46 **Protective** Monkey

CHARACTER RELATIONSHIPS

Percentage shows how easily a Monkey communicates with:

Easy Communication		Stressful	
PEGASUS	100%	TANUKI	5%
WOLF	90%	BLACK PANTHER	15%
ELEPHANT	85%	SHEEP	25%
KOALA	75%	FAWN	35%
CHEETAH	70%	TIGER	45%
MONKEY	60%	LION	55%

TIPS & TABOOS: Understanding a Monkey

Words & phrases	Utilize rather exaggerated expressions such as "Wow, that's interesting!" or "Amazing!"
Places for a date	Playful, fun places such as a game center or amusement park.
Great gift ideas	Small presents one at a time, rather than one expensive gift.
Communication	Gather and exchange useful information such as tips on discount shops and vouchers.
Caution: Taboos	Uninterested in the years ahead. Must talk with direct eye contact.

Quick-witted and good at sports, you are skilled at cheering up others. Since you are kind and caring, you are also a good teacher. Your face often shows what you are thinking, and this simplicity is loved by others. You are openhearted and can quickly patch up a quarrel by communicating your thoughts and feelings. You have a strong will to stand on your own two feet. If there is something that interests you, try to study it with dedication: this will help you become more mature. You have an outstanding ability to concentrate and a strong will to win. Although you are not very patient in overcoming hardships, if you keep on trying, you will have a greater chance of succeeding. You have no worries about money but since you tend to be weak in calculating profit and loss, you are not well suited for a career in business. On the other hand, having a superior sense for aesthetics, you would do well in creative work.

SUCCESS & LUCK: Your Rhythm of Fortune

Know the best time to plan for finance, career, love and more.

🔟 **Perfection**: You will be successful in everything

9️⃣ **Success**: Your best time for finance and competition

8️⃣ **Investment**: A good time for networking and money

7️⃣ **Change**: The right time to start something new

6️⃣ **Learning**: A time for studies and test-taking

5️⃣ **Action**: Make your move while in good health

4️⃣ **Balance**: Organize for harmony

3️⃣ **Arrangement**: Clean up the clutter in your life

2️⃣ **Waste**: You tend to waste your time, energy and money

1️⃣ **Caution**: Be careful in every way, especially when you are communicating with others

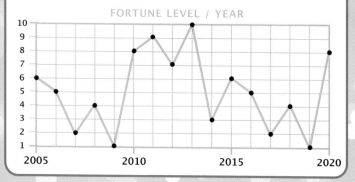

FORTUNE LEVEL / YEAR

♂ Has his own taste in fashion and trends

♀ Popular, cheerful and good at everything

Famous Restless Monkeys:

Mark Twain 11/30/1835
Steven Spielberg 12/18/1946
Pamela Anderson 7/1/1967

9 Ambitious MONKEY

You are active and full of curiosity, eager to make strides not only toward work or study, but also for pleasure and hobby. Since you enjoy everything with a sense of playfulness, you often become an expert in a certain field without realizing it. You are always eager to put your large stock of ideas into practice, but don't do this impatiently. Remember, haste makes waste. Cheerful and frank, you make others happy even when you are not in good spirits. Though you are broad-minded and accepting of others, you are not good at making efforts to be accepted yourself. That is why you sometimes feel lonely inside. Try to open your heart at times, as others may feel you can be selfish, and show that you want to be understood. If you try to live without being afraid of making mistakes and not using dishonest tactics, things will turn out well.

SUCCESS & LUCK: Your Rhythm of Fortune

Know the best time to plan for finance, career, love and more.

⑩ Perfection: You will be successful in everything

⑨ Success: Your best time for finance and competition

⑧ Investment: A good time for networking and money

⑦ Change: The right time to start something new

⑥ Learning: A time for studies and test-taking

⑤ Action: Make your move while in good health

④ Balance: Organize for harmony

③ Arrangement: Clean up the clutter in your life

② Waste: You tend to waste your time, energy and money

① Caution: Be careful in every way, especially when you are communicating with others

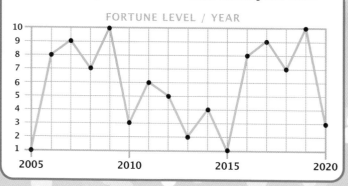

FORTUNE LEVEL / YEAR

♂ Generous and big-hearted

♀ Carefree and enjoys everything

Famous Ambitious Monkeys:

Bob Dylan 5/24/1941
Natalie Cole 2/6/1950
Hilary Swank 7/30/1974

51

15 Dignified MONKEY

By nature, you have a strong and unique intuition, which will sharpen as you experience life. You handle things cleverly, improve yourself very quickly and enjoy being ahead of the times. Cool and efficient, you reach your goal by taking the shortest route. You are very eager and ambitious to fulfill your life's goals, but being competitive and proud, you may sometimes be feared by others. You are very passionate in whatever you are facing, throwing all your heart and soul into it. You are the type who accumulates daily stresses to the boiling point. So do not overwork yourself, and be sure to blow off steam a little at a time. You have the ability to move people, and if you communicate with a warm and tolerant heart, possibilities will expand for your greater success.

SUCCESS & LUCK: Your Rhythm of Fortune

Know the best time to plan for finance, career, love and more.

⓾ Perfection: You will be successful in everything

➒ Success: Your best time for finance and competition

➑ Investment: A good time for networking and money

➐ Change: The right time to start something new

➏ Learning: A time for studies and test-taking

➎ Action: Make your move while in good health

➍ Balance: Organize for harmony

➌ Arrangement: Clean up the clutter in your life

➋ Waste: You tend to waste your time, energy and money

➊ Caution: Be careful in every way, especially when you are communicating with others

FORTUNE LEVEL / YEAR

 Really knows how to take chances

♀ Passionate, with a keen sense of beauty

Famous Dignified Monkeys:

Andy Warhol 8/6/1928
Whoopi Goldberg 11/13/1955
Sarah Jessica Parker 3/25/1965

53

Since you do not prefer a formal atmosphere, you like to be frank with others. It may be difficult for you to make friends because you are not skilled at expressing yourself. You are somewhat sensitive and often worry for no reason. But in time, your sophisticated intelligence and sense of humor will be understood and accepted. Although you hate to quarrel and never make unnecessary waves, you do not pander to the majority nor change your opinion. You act before you think, so your plans may be hit or miss. Clever and quick in understanding, you have the power with impressive concentration to carry out what seems impossible. Sometimes you sacrifice yourself for the sake of others. Naturally, your connections will expand, and before you realize it, you may be standing at the center of attention.

SUCCESS & LUCK: Your Rhythm of Fortune

Know the best time to plan for finance, career, love and more.

⑩ Perfection: You will be successful in everything

⑨ Success: Your best time for finance and competition

⑧ Investment: A good time for networking and money

❼ Change: The right time to start something new

❻ Learning: A time for studies and test-taking

❺ Action: Make your move while in good health

❹ Balance: Organize for harmony

❸ Arrangement: Clean up the clutter in your life

❷ Waste: You tend to waste your time, energy and money

❶ Caution: Be careful in every way, especially when you are communicating with others

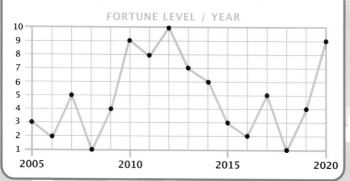

FORTUNE LEVEL / YEAR

 A fighter who stands up against the powers that be

 Charismatic and naturally attracts people

Famous Playful Monkeys:

Alexander Graham Bell 3/3/1847

Rita Hayworth. 10/17/1918

Queen Latifah 3/18/1970

55

Having a strong intuition by nature, you are very good at understanding others' feelings. Since you care for those around you and always work hard, you can be too delicate at times. You rarely show your feelings. Because you are not emotional and can think in a rational way, you work at your own pace very smoothly. Having an independent mind, you are skilled at analyzing the best timing to take action. But since you can handle things cleverly and shrewdly, you cannot leave things to others and thus tend to be weak at teamwork. You have the ability to create something from a formless idea, and you are a genius at making money. Although you do not live in luxury, you know how to utilize money to meet your needs.

SUCCESS & LUCK: Your Rhythm of Fortune

Know the best time to plan for finance, career, love and more.

⑩ Perfection: You will be successful in everything

⑨ Success: Your best time for finance and competition

⑧ Investment: A good time for networking and money

❼ Change: The right time to start something new

❻ Learning: A time for studies and test-taking

❺ Action: Make your move while in good health

❹ Balance: Organize for harmony

❸ Arrangement: Clean up the clutter in your life

❷ Waste: You tend to waste your time, energy and money

❶ Caution: Be careful in every way, especially when you are communicating with others

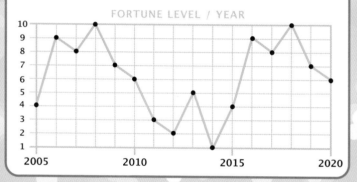

FORTUNE LEVEL / YEAR

A hard worker who likes to be praised

Generous, motherly and likes to do things for others

Famous Devoted Monkeys:

B.B. King 9/16/1925
Elton John 3/25/1947
Catherine Zeta-Jones 9/25/1969

46 Protective MONKEY

Since you are skilled at understanding others' feelings, you can relate to many people of all ages. Although you appear bright and cheerful and unconcerned with small matters, you are somewhat sensitive and proud. Since you are unyielding and try to keep up with the times, you tend to overextend yourself and do things beyond your ability. But you are a solid person who lives without daring adventures or big ups and downs. You are well suited for a career as an assistant, supporting others from behind the scenes rather than taking the lead. You treasure the things in your life that have practical value, even if they are hobbies. Eager to improve yourself, you continue moving forward carefully and patiently. But be sure to have sturdy prospects for the future, and try not to think only in the short term.

SUCCESS & LUCK: Your Rhythm of Fortune

Know the best time to plan for finance, career, love and more.

⑩ Perfection: You will be successful in everything

⑨ Success: Your best time for finance and competition

⑧ Investment: A good time for networking and money

⑦ Change: The right time to start something new

⑥ Learning: A time for studies and test-taking

⑤ Action: Make your move while in good health

④ Balance: Organize for harmony

③ Arrangement: Clean up the clutter in your life

② Waste: You tend to waste your time, energy and money

① Caution: Be careful in every way, especially when you are communicating with others

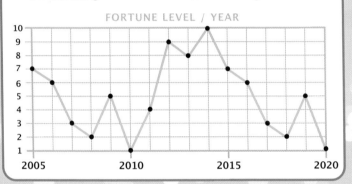

FORTUNE LEVEL / YEAR

♂ Logical, with stylish and refined manners

♀ Hardworking, cheers up others and lives a fulfilling life

Famous Protective Monkeys:

Judy Garland 6/10/1922
Audrey Hepburn 5/4/1929
Andy Garcia 4/12/1956

CHEETAH

- have an extremely positive mind
- not concerned with small matters
- a good sprinter, but with power that does not last
- want to be the center of attention
- buy things as soon as you desire, without hesitation
- big talker with a big attitude
- like to eat Korean BBQ

. . . .

1 **Marathon** Cheetah

7 **Sprinting** Cheetah

42 **Tough** Cheetah

48 **Graceful** Cheetah

CHARACTER RELATIONSHIPS

Percentage shows how easily a Cheetah communicates with:

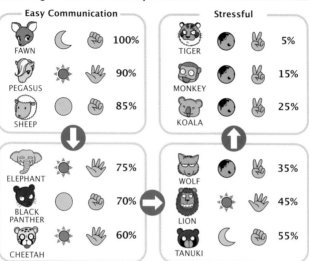

Easy Communication		Stressful	
FAWN	100%	TIGER	5%
PEGASUS	90%	MONKEY	15%
SHEEP	85%	KOALA	25%
ELEPHANT	75%	WOLF	35%
BLACK PANTHER	70%	LION	45%
CHEETAH	60%	TANUKI	55%

TIPS & TABOOS: Understanding a Cheetah

Words & phrases
Praise their abilities with phrases like "You're a success!" and "You took swift action."

Places for a date
Popular and famous locations seen in movies and TV shows, and interactive, fun places (e.g., Korean BBQ restaurants).

Great gift ideas
Popular, brand-name goods. They also enjoy presents from abroad.

Communication
Talk about love and sexual topics. Thrilling stories are their favorite topic.

Caution: Taboos
Hate to hear complaints. Saying "Didn't you know?" to them is taboo.

Since you are honest and sincere, friendly and innocent, you will maintain your youthful appearance, even as you grow older. Your sophisticated manners and attractive air are your charming points that are intriguing to the opposite sex. Idealistic and having a strong sense to fight against injustice, you hate vagueness and try to define clearly what is right and wrong in every situation. Because of your high self-esteem, you might be taken as an impudent, overconfident person. You are quite careful with money. Although skilled at taking quick action, you sometimes lack the patience and persistence to overcome difficulties. You are gifted with social success, so if you maintain good relations with others and try not to be too dogmatic, you will lead a life of favor.

SUCCESS & LUCK: Your Rhythm of Fortune

Know the best time to plan for finance, career, love and more.

⑩ Perfection: You will be successful in everything

⑨ Success: Your best time for finance and competition

⑧ Investment: A good time for networking and money

⑦ Change: The right time to start something new

⑥ Learning: A time for studies and test-taking

⑤ Action: Make your move while in good health

④ Balance: Organize for harmony

③ Arrangement: Clean up the clutter in your life

② Waste: You tend to waste your time, energy and money

① Caution: Be careful in every way, especially when you are communicating with others

FORTUNE LEVEL / YEAR

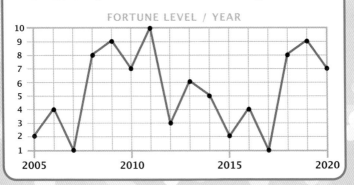

 Nice and attractive, with a charming and innocent nature

Always chasing after a dream and romance and hates to be alone

Famous Marathon Cheetahs:

Mother Teresa. 8/27/1910

David Hasselhoff. 7/17/1952

Keira Knightley 3/26/1985

You give a somewhat delicate, tense and attentive impression with a noble air. You are very competitive and have a strong sense of justice that compels you to fight against the powers that be. Your appearance is elegant and gentle, but in fact you are stubborn and have a straight-forward character. You are original and have a strong sense of analysis. Since you hate to compromise, you often have conflicts with others. You should sometimes withdraw and be considerate, playing a supportive role. You change your mind very quickly, and you can be practical in recognizing the difference between fantasy and reality. You want to play an active role in the global community and wish to lead a dynamic life. Because of this, there might be big changes in your life, such as shifts in career or housing, but you can handle these transitions well.

SUCCESS & LUCK: Your Rhythm of Fortune

Know the best time to plan for finance, career, love and more.

⑩ Perfection: You will be successful in everything

⑨ Success: Your best time for finance and competition

⑧ Investment: A good time for networking and money

⑦ Change: The right time to start something new

⑥ Learning: A time for studies and test-taking

⑤ Action: Make your move while in good health

④ Balance: Organize for harmony

③ Arrangement: Clean up the clutter in your life

② Waste: You tend to waste your time, energy and money

① Caution: Be careful in every way, especially when you are communicating with others

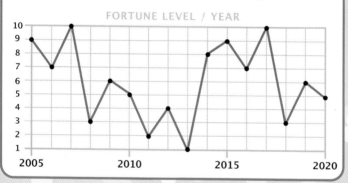

FORTUNE LEVEL / YEAR

♂ An adventurer with an ambitious mind

♀ A hard worker with a very positive mind

Famous Sprinting Cheetahs:

Margaret Thatcher 10/13/1925
Renée Zellweger 4/25/1969
Orlando Bloom 1/13/1977

Since you are a quick worker, you act as soon as you think. Short-tempered, you are brisk and have the passion to forge ahead toward your goals. You are also fashionable and care about your appearance. Being rather competitive and saying things in a straightforward manner, you tend to make both friends and enemies, but you try hard to make friends who will support you. You are outstandingly clever, and your intuition with people and your refined persuasive speaking skills are your protective strengths. You not only chase your dreams but can steadily calculate your ideas, so you will never make emotional decisions based only on your likes and dislikes, nor ignore profit and loss. You are weak, however, in long-term work and tend to be too optimistic. Since you face your ideals with innate activeness and intuition, you will gain a good reputation in business.

SUCCESS & LUCK: Your Rhythm of Fortune

Know the best time to plan for finance, career, love and more.

10 Perfection: You will be successful in everything

9 Success: Your best time for finance and competition

8 Investment: A good time for networking and money

7 Change: The right time to start something new

6 Learning: A time for studies and test-taking

5 Action: Make your move while in good health

4 Balance: Organize for harmony

3 Arrangement: Clean up the clutter in your life

2 Waste: You tend to waste your time, energy and money

1 Caution: Be careful in every way, especially when you are communicating with others

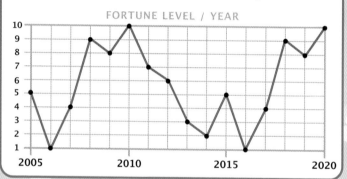

FORTUNE LEVEL / YEAR

♂ Steady and business-minded

♀ Forges ahead toward her dream

Famous Tough Cheetahs:

Walter Cronkite 11/4/1916
John Travolta 2/18/1954
Halle Berry 8/14/1966

Graceful
CHEETAH

An open-minded sociable type, you can be candid with anyone. You have clear likes and dislikes and are often outspoken; you are also somewhat aggressive and competitive. Since you act according to your intuition, you tend to be hasty, but that is part of your lovable charm. Warmhearted and humane, you know how to connect with others. By nature, you are a person who puts forth much effort. You will devote yourself to anything in order to achieve your purpose and make things go well. You are a skilled speaker and a good worker, but when you are not in good spirits, you can be a slow starter. And if you lose sight of your purpose, you might become detached from reality. Since you tend to make subjective decisions, it is always important to keep calm and composed.

SUCCESS & LUCK: Your Rhythm of Fortune

Know the best time to plan for finance, career, love and more.

❿ Perfection: You will be successful in everything

❾ Success: Your best time for finance and competition

❽ Investment: A good time for networking and money

❼ Change: The right time to start something new

❻ Learning: A time for studies and test-taking

❺ Action: Make your move while in good health

❹ Balance: Organize for harmony

❸ Arrangement: Clean up the clutter in your life

❷ Waste: You tend to waste your time, energy and money

❶ Caution: Be careful in every way, especially when you are communicating with others

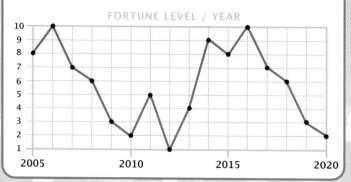

FORTUNE LEVEL / YEAR

♂ Passionate, affectionate and easily moved to tears

♀ An inventor with a rich sense of humor

Famous Graceful Cheetahs:

Leonardo da Vinci 4/15/1452

Ringo Starr 7/7/1940

Susan Sarandon 10/4/1946

BLACK PANTHER

- like "new" things
- want to be cool, sophisticated and trendy
- aggressive but lack perseverance

- weak in handling unexpected difficulties
- like black and white colors
- very sensitive
- want to hold a leading position

- -

5 **Caring** Black Panther

44 **Passionate** Black Panther

50 **Sentimental** Black Panther

53 **Soulful** Black Panther

56 **Friendly** Black Panther

59 **Freedom-Loving** Black Panther

CHARACTER RELATIONSHIPS

Percentage shows how easily a Black Panther communicates with:

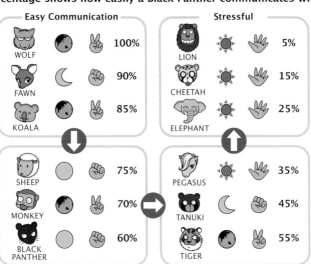

Easy Communication		Stressful	
WOLF	100%	LION	5%
FAWN	90%	CHEETAH	15%
KOALA	85%	ELEPHANT	25%
SHEEP	75%	PEGASUS	35%
MONKEY	70%	TANUKI	45%
BLACK PANTHER	60%	TIGER	55%

TIPS & TABOOS: Understanding a Black Panther

Words & phrases	Admire their sensibilities with "You have good taste" and "Cool!"
Places for a date	Places known only by the hippest trend seekers. They also enjoy stylish shops and trendy locations.
Great gift ideas	Anything in line with the latest trends. Gifts should be "cutting edge."
Communication	Discuss new products and cutting-edge information. They are delighted to catch new trends early on.
Caution: Taboos	Don't talk in a commanding or authoritative tone. Saying "You don't look cool" is taboo.

71

5 Caring
BLACK PANTHER

You have a stylish manner and a bright, cheerful character, and you aren't concerned with small matters. You are an optimist who thinks it's natural that everyone shows such an interest in you, and truly, this innocence is loved by many. Although appearing gentle, you are quite competitive and have strong willpower and pride. You are weak in making quick decisions and determining what is right or wrong. But having refined sensibilities, you are good at showing your artistic talents. Since you are not skilled at understanding others' feelings, your communication might be a bit weak. But you are very independent and strong enough to work alone, so if you continue working diligently, you will naturally be supported by others as a leader.

SUCCESS & LUCK: Your Rhythm of Fortune

Know the best time to plan for finance, career, love and more.

10 **Perfection**: You will be successful in everything

9 **Success**: Your best time for finance and competition

8 **Investment**: A good time for networking and money

7 **Change**: The right time to start something new

6 **Learning**: A time for studies and test-taking

5 **Action**: Make your move while in good health

4 **Balance**: Organize for harmony

3 **Arrangement**: Clean up the clutter in your life

2 **Waste**: You tend to waste your time, energy and money

1 **Caution**: Be careful in every way, especially when you are communicating with others

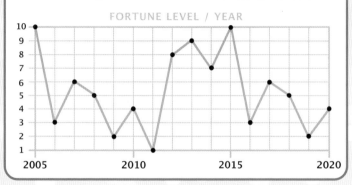

FORTUNE LEVEL / YEAR

 Artistic, with a stylish and fashionable appearance

♀ A trend catcher who lives life at her own pace

Famous Caring Black Panthers:

Nat King Cole 3/17/1919
Hugh Hefner 4/9/1926
Earvin "Magic" Johnson 8/14/1959

You are a steady, passionate person, but you appear modest and have a gentle manner. Since you are moody and experience big ups and downs, you might feel a gap between your ideal and reality. Sometimes your actions might not be understood by others, so be careful not to reflect your fitfulness in your work. You are sociable, eager and skilled at taking action, clever at anything you attempt. An intelligent person, you catch on to new trends and often talk about things others have not heard of yet. Having high self-esteem, you wish to have people's favor, but you do not always lay the groundwork for it. Your guiding principle is to make steady efforts. You are gifted with a strong power of verbal persuasion.

SUCCESS & LUCK: Your Rhythm of Fortune

Know the best time to plan for finance, career, love and more.

⑩ Perfection: You will be successful in everything

⑨ Success: Your best time for finance and competition

⑧ Investment: A good time for networking and money

❼ Change: The right time to start something new

❻ Learning: A time for studies and test-taking

❺ Action: Make your move while in good health

❹ Balance: Organize for harmony

❸ Arrangement: Clean up the clutter in your life

❷ Waste: You tend to waste your time, energy and money

❶ Caution: Be careful in every way, especially when you are communicating with others

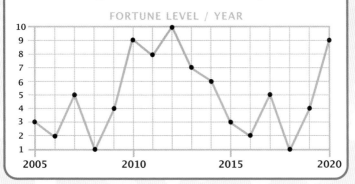

FORTUNE LEVEL / YEAR

 Has keen senses, enjoys excitement and watches the latest trends

 Modest and graceful, with great inner passion

Famous Passionate Black Panthers:

Johann Sebastian Bach 3/21/1685

Sean Connery 8/25/1930

Robert De Niro 8/17/1943

50 Sentimental
BLACK PANTHER

You appear mature and gentle, but inside, you are strong-willed. Sometimes you get so stubborn that you shut your ears to others' advice. Although you might lack the skills of calmness and cool analysis, you have strong intuition and a flexible mind to see the world and keep up with the times, so you can manage to get through the difficulties in your life. Since you are quick-witted, you can adapt to any circumstance, but be careful not to be taken as "everybody's friend." An active person who values the power of inspiration, you may appear inconsistent and unrestrained. In spite of your warm character, you worry and frequently struggle with mental conflicts. If you realize this and accept it, you can get past this self-contradiction. You are a hardworking person with an independent mind and can show yourself boldly at work.

SUCCESS & LUCK: Your Rhythm of Fortune

Know the best time to plan for finance, career, love and more.

⑩ Perfection: You will be successful in everything

⑨ Success: Your best time for finance and competition

⑧ Investment: A good time for networking and money

❼ Change: The right time to start something new

❻ Learning: A time for studies and test-taking

❺ Action: Make your move while in good health

❹ Balance: Organize for harmony

❸ Arrangement: Clean up the clutter in your life

❷ Waste: You tend to waste your time, energy and money

❶ Caution: Be careful in every way, especially when you are communicating with others

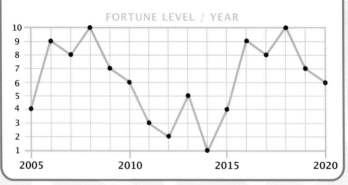

FORTUNE LEVEL / YEAR

♂ Highly motivated with keen foresight

♀ Hardworking, with a good sense for taking chances

Famous Sentimental Black Panthers:

Alfred Hitchcock 8/13/1899

Natalie Wood. 7/20/1938

Demi Moore 11/11/1962

You are pure and gentle but rather delicate, and give the impression of lacking a sense of reality. Very shy, you are weak in conversing with new acquaintances, but you are quick-witted and forward thinking. You are able to show your talents utilizing your strong artistic sense. With your cleverness and efforts, you can handle things very well, but since you are a moody person, you soon lose interest or tire of something, even when you are only halfway through. Because of this, you are not particularly well suited for teamwork. You have clear likes and dislikes and hate to be under anyone's thumb. Since you always hold youthful ideals with a pure heart, you never doubt people's goodwill. Your earnestness in acknowledging your own faults and improving yourself is also your charm.

SUCCESS & LUCK: Your Rhythm of Fortune

Know the best time to plan for finance, career, love and more.

🔟 **Perfection**: You will be successful in everything

9️⃣ **Success**: Your best time for finance and competition

8️⃣ **Investment**: A good time for networking and money

7️⃣ **Change**: The right time to start something new

6️⃣ **Learning**: A time for studies and test-taking

5️⃣ **Action**: Make your move while in good health

4️⃣ **Balance**: Organize for harmony

3️⃣ **Arrangement**: Clean up the clutter in your life

2️⃣ **Waste**: You tend to waste your time, energy and money

1️⃣ **Caution**: Be careful in every way, especially when you are communicating with others

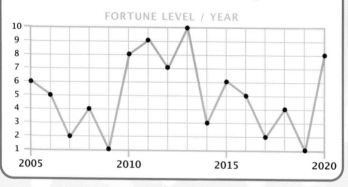

FORTUNE LEVEL / YEAR

♂ A genius with a pure heart

♀ A dreamer with a pure heart who enjoys whimsical things

Famous Soulful Black Panthers:

Grace Kelly 11/12/1928
Russell Crowe 4/7/1964
Leonardo Di Caprio 11/11/1974

You are an honest person who is sincere with everyone, and you communicate in a flexible manner. Even if something concerns your own interests, you can judge the situation with a neutral mind. Although warmhearted and tolerant, you don't welcome others into your world, so you might not have a wide circle of friends. You are the type who cherishes long-lasting relationships with a few compatible friends. You always have unfulfilled dreams to fuel your motivations. Being rather impatient, you hate to stay still and can hardly wait to take action as soon as you have your mind set, but you also have a strong will to finish something by yourself. Since you have a keen sense of beauty and color, you can utilize this innate ability in fashion or interior design.

SUCCESS & LUCK: Your Rhythm of Fortune

Know the best time to plan for finance, career, love and more.

⑩ Perfection: You will be successful in everything

⑨ Success: Your best time for finance and competition

⑧ Investment: A good time for networking and money

❼ Change: The right time to start something new

❻ Learning: A time for studies and test-taking

❺ Action: Make your move while in good health

❹ Balance: Organize for harmony

❸ Arrangement: Clean up the clutter in your life

❷ Waste: You tend to waste your time, energy and money

❶ Caution: Be careful in every way, especially when you are communicating with others

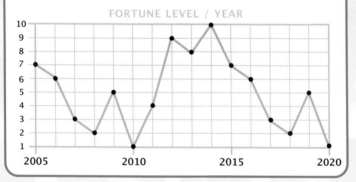

FORTUNE LEVEL / YEAR

♂ Simplistic and wishes to live as he is

♀ Gentle, kind and tends to be reckless

Famous Friendly Black Panthers:

Abraham Lincoln. 2/12/1809
Charles Darwin 2/12/1809
Ashley Judd. 4/19/1968

You are a polite, calm and gentle person. Since you take action only after thorough consideration, you don't make silly, careless mistakes. A person of few words, you live by the saying, "Actions speak louder than words." You are not skilled at explaining things in a logical manner, but with your keen intuition, you can discern the thoughts of those around you, and you intuitively know what to do next. You keep your emotions in good balance with reason. But sometimes, you depend on your moody likes and dislikes or make decisions on a whim, so you are weak in analyzing objectively. You tend to have good luck with business opportunities through friends and colleagues. You should have a good advisor in case you have hesitations while making your own decisions.

SUCCESS & LUCK: Your Rhythm of Fortune

Know the best time to plan for finance, career, love and more.

⑩ Perfection: You will be successful in everything

⑨ Success: Your best time for finance and competition

⑧ Investment: A good time for networking and money

⑦ Change: The right time to start something new

⑥ Learning: A time for studies and test-taking

⑤ Action: Make your move while in good health

④ Balance: Organize for harmony

③ Arrangement: Clean up the clutter in your life

② Waste: You tend to waste your time, energy and money

① Caution: Be careful in every way, especially when you are communicating with others

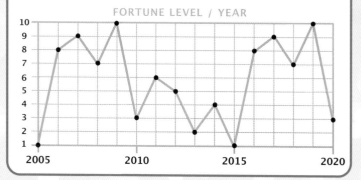

FORTUNE LEVEL / YEAR

 Romantic and full of emotions

 Peace-loving and faces up to reality

Famous Freedom–Loving Black Panthers:

Charlie Chaplin 4/16/1889

Bill Gates 10/28/1955

Gwyneth Paltrow 9/28/1972

LION

- do not whine

- place importance on courtesy and politeness

- care much about public image

- enjoy being treated like royalty or a VIP

- very strict teaching style

- tend to be kind to yourself but strict with others

- act like a spoiled child at home

- -

51 **Independent** Lion

52 **Captain** Lion

57 **Emotional** Lion

58 **Sensitive** Lion

CHARACTER RELATIONSHIPS

Percentage shows how easily a Lion communicates with:

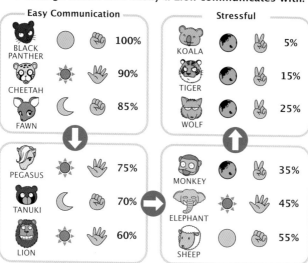

Easy Communication			Stressful		
BLACK PANTHER		100%	KOALA		5%
CHEETAH		90%	TIGER		15%
FAWN		85%	WOLF		25%
PEGASUS		75%	MONKEY		35%
TANUKI		70%	ELEPHANT		45%
LION		60%	SHEEP		55%

TIPS & TABOOS: Understanding a Lion

Words & phrases
Emphasize their special treatment with "You're a leader" and "You are a VIP."

Places for a date
Beautiful, luxurious places or a spot with a pleasant night view.

Great gift ideas
Something from one of the world's top brands, even if it is a small item.

Communication
Talk endlessly about the entertainment world and TV shows.

Caution: Taboos
Too much frankness in the beginning, or a conversation lacking politeness, is not good. Bragging to them is taboo.

51 Independent LION

Having strong willpower, you never whine or complain. You are strict with yourself as well as those around you. To others, you appear sociable, but you are by nature fearless of being alone and have a spirit of independence to create your own future. Since you are competitive and patient and prefer to take care of yourself, you do not expect others to help you. Very cautious and rarely mentioning your real intentions, you have a hard time opening up to others. You are a leader and strict teacher, and you are very observant and notice every little thing. So if someone can endure this strictness, you will lead a wonderful "mentor and pupil" relationship. With steady efforts, you can achieve your intended results, but you are weak in cooperating with others at work. If you always remember to be cooperative, you can make the most of your innate power of good fortune.

SUCCESS & LUCK: Your Rhythm of Fortune

Know the best time to plan for finance, career, love and more.

10 Perfection: You will be successful in everything

9 Success: Your best time for finance and competition

8 Investment: A good time for networking and money

7 Change: The right time to start something new

6 Learning: A time for studies and test-taking

5 Action: Make your move while in good health

4 Balance: Organize for harmony

3 Arrangement: Clean up the clutter in your life

2 Waste: You tend to waste your time, energy and money

1 Caution: Be careful in every way, especially when you are communicating with others

FORTUNE LEVEL / YEAR

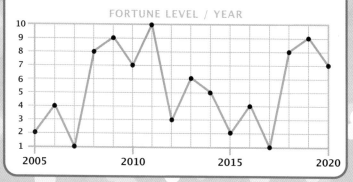

 Wants to do things his own way

Likes to be perfect and never compromises

Famous Independent Lions:

Louis Armstrong 8/4/1901

Kiefer Sutherland 12/21/1966

Katie Holmes 12/18/1978

Since your high self-esteem is not evident to others, you appear modest and gentle. A neat and elegant person, you are gifted at brightening up the room. Since you are very cautious, you rarely show your thoughts and emotions. You just listen quietly to what others say, but in your heart, you tend to think that you are the one who knows what's right. Being strict with your family and close friends is your way of showing affection, and you do not make compromises. Although you make decisions steadily and rationally, you are rather argumentative and have a difficult temperament. It may be hard for you to adapt to new circumstances, so you tend to be passive at first. But after you adjust, you begin to make assertions and show your leadership. This comes from your simplicity, however, and not from ambition.

SUCCESS & LUCK: Your Rhythm of Fortune

Know the best time to plan for finance, career, love and more.

⑩ Perfection: You will be successful in everything

⑨ Success: Your best time for finance and competition

⑧ Investment: A good time for networking and money

⑦ Change: The right time to start something new

⑥ Learning: A time for studies and test-taking

⑤ Action: Make your move while in good health

④ Balance: Organize for harmony

③ Arrangement: Clean up the clutter in your life

② Waste: You tend to waste your time, energy and money

① Caution: Be careful in every way, especially when you are communicating with others

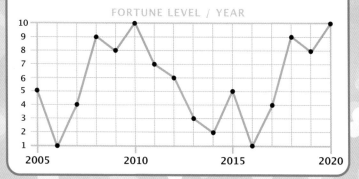

FORTUNE LEVEL / YEAR

♂ Neat and careful, with good manners

♀ Gentle, with the ability to be the leader of a group

Famous Captain Lions:

Yoko Ono 2/18/1933
Ted Turner 11/19/1938
Jim Carrey 1/17/1962

You are sincere and have regard for others but find it difficult to be affable or give compliments. You appear sociable, but in fact you are quite competitive and hate to fall behind the competition. Having a straightforward character, your frankness may be accepted with favor. You can show your sense of humor in front of close friends, but when you are at work you are drastically severe to yourself as well as to others and never allow compromises. Since you do not take advantage of situations and are not a strategic thinker, you might be losing out on some opportunities. Strong with numbers and analysis, you are well suited for a career in accounting. What you establish in a long period of time will remain for future generations. Having a strong sense of justice, you have the kindness to assist the needy or helpless at any cost. You take good care of others and show outstanding leadership skills.

SUCCESS & LUCK: Your Rhythm of Fortune

Know the best time to plan for finance, career, love and more.

⑩ Perfection: You will be successful in everything

⑨ Success: Your best time for finance and competition

⑧ Investment: A good time for networking and money

⑦ Change: The right time to start something new

⑥ Learning: A time for studies and test-taking

⑤ Action: Make your move while in good health

④ Balance: Organize for harmony

③ Arrangement: Clean up the clutter in your life

② Waste: You tend to waste your time, energy and money

① Caution: Be careful in every way, especially when you are communicating with others

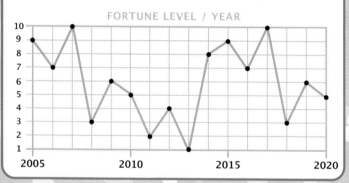

FORTUNE LEVEL / YEAR

Skilled at analyzing what is right and wrong

Intelligent and in control of her emotions

Famous Emotional Lions:

Sir Isaac Newton 12/25/1642

Vanessa Williams 3/18/1963

Charlie Sheen 9/3/1965

You give the impression of being a carefree, generous and understanding person; but in fact, you hold the strong conviction that your heart will never be moved except by what you believe in. You value authority and also hate anything that disturbs the peace. Even when in trouble, you do not depend on others and try to resolve the situation by yourself. Although you are intelligent and have strengths in various fields, you tend to care too much about external circumstances and therefore meddle with things. Having high self-esteem, you will be hurt by even the slightest unfavorable words spoken about you. You are a steady and intelligent type who determines the next step based on various data—and not by intuition or inspiration. You may not live a calm life but can overcome any situation with your innate strength and good luck.

SUCCESS & LUCK: Your Rhythm of Fortune

Know the best time to plan for finance, career, love and more.

⓾ Perfection: You will be successful in everything

❾ Success: Your best time for finance and competition

❽ Investment: A good time for networking and money

❼ Change: The right time to start something new

❻ Learning: A time for studies and test-taking

❺ Action: Make your move while in good health

❹ Balance: Organize for harmony

❸ Arrangement: Clean up the clutter in your life

❷ Waste: You tend to waste your time, energy and money

❶ Caution: Be careful in every way, especially when you are communicating with others

FORTUNE LEVEL / YEAR

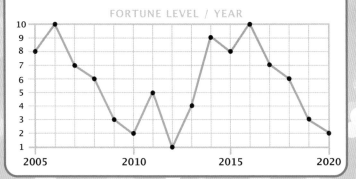

 Has strong moral sense and a noble and pure character

 Gentle but tough-minded

Famous Sensitive Lions:

Marilyn Monroe. 6/1/1926

Luciano Pavarotti. 10/12/1935

Jodie Foster. 11/19/1962

93

TIGER

- have a great sense of mental and physical balance
- sensitive to others' words
- need to have the overall view of a situation
- take action only after careful consideration

- like colorful things
- equal and humanitarian personality who is often a leader
- can say harsh things with a smile on your face

- -

6 **Affectionate** Tiger

43 **Energetic** Tiger

49 **Confident** Tiger

54 **Optimistic** Tiger

55 **Powerful** Tiger

60 **Liberty** Tiger

CHARACTER RELATIONSHIPS

Percentage shows how easily a Tiger communicates with:

Easy Communication

CHEETAH		100%
MONKEY		90%
PEGASUS		85%

WOLF		75%
LION		70%
TIGER		60%

Stressful

SHEEP		5%
TANUKI		15%
FAWN		25%

BLACK PANTHER		35%
KOALA		45%
ELEPHANT		55%

TIPS & TABOOS: Understanding a Tiger

Words & phrases	Praise their good personality by saying "I depend on you" and "We respect you."
Places for a date	Places that are just right for taking a drive, going to dinner, etc. Having a perfect plan for the outing is key.
Great gift ideas	Colorful objects and clothes. Sunglasses are a good choice.
Communication	Enjoy talking at length about their clothes and accessories. They will be delighted to answer questions.
Caution: Taboos	Do not push for an immediate decision. They tend to get annoyed about the way of expression rather than the topic itself.

6 Affectionate TIGER

You are a gentle optimist with a tolerant mind. Having a bright and active personality, you are a sociable, well-respected person who is willing to help the needy. You have high self-esteem and do not like to be subordinate to anyone. Since you are not shy and can steadily calculate profit and loss, you are likely to be an important leader. Although you are a humanitarian with a strong sense of justice, you tend to be easy on people, as well as yourself, in a careless manner. You are physically and mentally tough and have great strength. In spite of your ability to make objective decisions, you can be rather weak on making them quickly. Since you are adaptable and faithful to your inner voice, you never regret nor bear a grudge against anyone.

SUCCESS & LUCK: Your Rhythm of Fortune

Know the best time to plan for finance, career, love and more.

⑩ Perfection: You will be successful in everything

⑨ Success: Your best time for finance and competition

⑧ Investment: A good time for networking and money

⑦ Change: The right time to start something new

⑥ Learning: A time for studies and test-taking

⑤ Action: Make your move while in good health

④ Balance: Organize for harmony

③ Arrangement: Clean up the clutter in your life

② Waste: You tend to waste your time, energy and money

① Caution: Be careful in every way, especially when you are communicating with others

FORTUNE LEVEL / YEAR

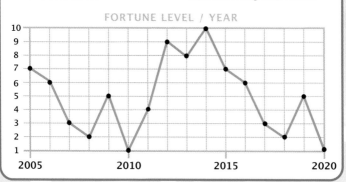

 Gentle, steady and reliable

♀ Warmhearted, with a strong mind

Famous Affectionate Tigers:

Charles Dickens 2/7/1812
Sidney Poitier 2/20/1924
James Brown 5/3/1933

43 Energetic TIGER

Y ou appear calm and composed, living life at your own pace. But secretly, you have delicate sensibilities and keen, observant eyes. You are a tidy person and are very good at organizing messes. You have a noble character, sincere and devoted to everyone, but as you require the same sincerity from others, you tend to be strict with them. You judge others by your own standards and tend to be stubborn in asserting yourself. You shouldn't adhere only to your own ideas and opinions. Be broad-minded and always remember to keep your innate sense of good balance. Having strong leadership qualities, you like to take care of others but hate to be under somebody's direction or to be taken care of. Since you have good luck, there will always be someone to help you when you are facing difficult times.

SUCCESS & LUCK: Your Rhythm of Fortune

Know the best time to plan for finance, career, love and more.

🔟 Perfection: You will be successful in everything

➒ Success: Your best time for finance and competition

➑ Investment: A good time for networking and money

➐ Change: The right time to start something new

➏ Learning: A time for studies and test-taking

➎ Action: Make your move while in good health

➍ Balance: Organize for harmony

➌ Arrangement: Clean up the clutter in your life

➋ Waste: You tend to waste your time, energy and money

➊ Caution: Be careful in every way, especially when you are communicating with others

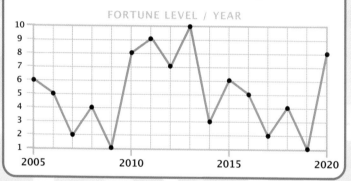

FORTUNE LEVEL / YEAR

♂ Logical, with a quick mind

♀ Hardworking, with a frank character

Famous Energetic Tigers:

William Shakespeare 4/23/1564
Dennis Rodman. 5/13/1961
Mariah Carey. 3/27/1970

49 Confident TIGER

You are vigorous and friendly, never too cautious or flattering. You are also broad-minded, and your caring generosity is your charm. At first sight, you may seem rather unapproachable, but you really are a polite and sincere person. Very good at making friends and expanding your social circle, you maintain good relations with everyone. You are a well-balanced person who isn't influenced by circumstances. You are quick-witted and accurate in judging situations and observing people, but sometimes you think too much and wonder which is the right decision. Having clear likes and dislikes, as well as keen sensibilities, you can sometimes be over-anxious. But since you are optimistic, you do not worry too much. As you are a positive person, you recover quickly, even when you get depressed.

SUCCESS & LUCK: Your Rhythm of Fortune

Know the best time to plan for finance, career, love and more.

🔟 Perfection: You will be successful in everything

9️ Success: Your best time for finance and competition

8️ Investment: A good time for networking and money

7️ Change: The right time to start something new

6️ Learning: A time for studies and test-taking

5️ Action: Make your move while in good health

4️ Balance: Organize for harmony

3️ Arrangement: Clean up the clutter in your life

2️ Waste: You tend to waste your time, energy and money

1️ Caution: Be careful in every way, especially when you are communicating with others

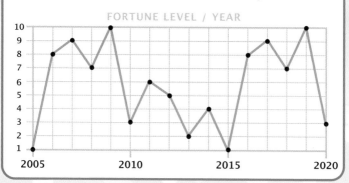

FORTUNE LEVEL / YEAR

♂ Well-balanced and pays careful attention to others

♀ Sociable and clever, with a "big-sister" personality

Famous Confident Tigers:

Marlon Brando 4/3/1924

Chuck Norris 3/10/1940

Tatum O'Neal 11/5/1963

You are a frank person who can be equally friendly with everyone. Although strict with yourself, you are soft on others. So people often come to you for advice, and you cannot refuse them because of your volunteering spirit. Be careful not to lose yourself while concentrating on problems that are not your own. Your insight into human relations is not so keen, but you can always observe with fairness, without holding prejudices. Since you are very gentle, you tend to believe what you see and hear without doubts. But given your innate stubbornness, you will never yield to unreasonable situations. Your life may be dramatic, with big ups and downs, but the more you experience failure and success, the more you will be respected.

SUCCESS & LUCK: Your Rhythm of Fortune

Know the best time to plan for finance, career, love and more.

10 Perfection: You will be successful in everything

9 Success: Your best time for finance and competition

8 Investment: A good time for networking and money

7 Change: The right time to start something new

6 Learning: A time for studies and test-taking

5 Action: Make your move while in good health

4 Balance: Organize for harmony

3 Arrangement: Clean up the clutter in your life

2 Waste: You tend to waste your time, energy and money

1 Caution: Be careful in every way, especially when you are communicating with others

FORTUNE LEVEL / YEAR

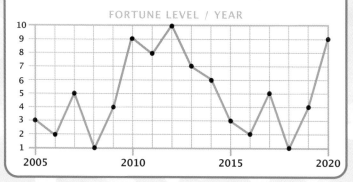

 Strong-willed and can make fair judgments

 Hardworking, with self-confidence and a big heart

Famous Optimistic Tigers:

Walt Disney. 12/5/1901

Juliette Binoche 3/9/1964

Jennifer Aniston 2/11/1969

55 Powerful TIGER

You appear mature because you have always been self-focused, but as you grow older, you will remain young and sociable. Since you are fearless, never flatter and express yourself in a logical and straightforward way, people respect your superiority. Idealistic and never accepting unreasonable situations, you have a fighting spirit to stand up against the powers that be to save the weak. When you overestimate yourself, you can come across as a "hero" and may end up feeling isolated. Be modest and strive for better communication. Quick-witted and very responsible, you are skilled at making decisions and putting them into practice, so you will be respected as a reliable person who takes action at the right time. The more you experience, the more you can develop the power to observe and analyze yourself and the world. You will be a late bloomer, succeeding in your later years.

SUCCESS & LUCK: Your Rhythm of Fortune

Know the best time to plan for finance, career, love and more.

⑩ Perfection: You will be successful in everything

⑨ Success: Your best time for finance and competition

⑧ Investment: A good time for networking and money

⑦ Change: The right time to start something new

⑥ Learning: A time for studies and test-taking

⑤ Action: Make your move while in good health

④ Balance: Organize for harmony

③ Arrangement: Clean up the clutter in your life

② Waste: You tend to waste your time, energy and money

① Caution: Be careful in every way, especially when you are communicating with others

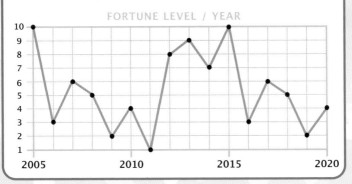

FORTUNE LEVEL / YEAR

 Has a rebellious spirit to fight against the powers that be

 Confident and has great energy to take action

Famous Powerful Tigers:

Elizabeth Taylor 2/27/1932

Denzel Washington 12/28/1954

Brett Favre 10/10/1969

Your impression is pure and innocent, and you attract attention from both sexes. You are warm and sincere, as well as kind and caring, but you tend to be flattered by praise and soft words, so be careful. You are quick-witted and can be flexible. Although carefree and rather sociable, you have high self-esteem and a noble mind that values honor. You treasure your own individual lifestyle. While living a steady life, you are a romanticist as well, reaching for your ideals. This youthful spirit of cherishing your dreams is your greatest charm. You will be more successful when you do what is requested by others—not moving too aggressively with your own intentions in mind. A passive attitude will be the key to opening the door to your success.

SUCCESS & LUCK: Your Rhythm of Fortune

Know the best time to plan for finance, career, love and more.

⑩ Perfection: You will be successful in everything

⑨ Success: Your best time for finance and competition

⑧ Investment: A good time for networking and money

❼ Change: The right time to start something new

❻ Learning: A time for studies and test-taking

❺ Action: Make your move while in good health

❹ Balance: Organize for harmony

❸ Arrangement: Clean up the clutter in your life

❷ Waste: You tend to waste your time, energy and money

❶ Caution: Be careful in every way, especially when you are communicating with others

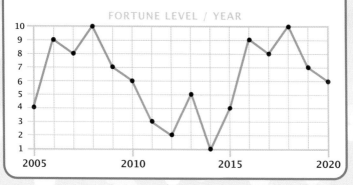

FORTUNE LEVEL / YEAR

♂ Has a charitable spirit of high ideals

♀ Bright, cheerful and likes to do things for others

Famous Liberty Tigers:

Steve Allen 12/26/1921
Jack Lemmon 2/8/1925
Jack Nicklaus 1/21/1940

TANUKI

- love Asian styles

- cherish traditional things

- regard experience and achievement as important

- can act as other animal characters

- adored by the elderly

- want to work for good relationships with others

- like to visit favorite places to shop

2 **Sociable** Tanuki

8 **Glorious** Tanuki

41 **Potential** Tanuki

47 **Mighty-Hearted** Tanuki

TANUKI: *The tanuki is an indigenous animal of Japan, similar to a raccoon or badger. Well known throughout Japan not only as a wild animal but also as a cultural figure, the tanuki often appears in folktales. Often compared to the fox, the tanuki is known for taking on the shape of other creatures or objects. While the fox is famous for its cunning character, the tanuki is jolly and somewhat gullible. It is widely accepted as a lovable creature.*

CHARACTER RELATIONSHIPS

Percentage shows how easily a Tanuki communicates with:

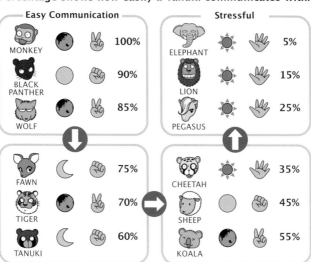

Easy Communication		Stressful	
MONKEY	100%	ELEPHANT	5%
BLACK PANTHER	90%	LION	15%
WOLF	85%	PEGASUS	25%
FAWN	75%	CHEETAH	35%
TIGER	70%	SHEEP	45%
TANUKI	60%	KOALA	55%

TIPS & TABOOS: Understanding a Tanuki

Words & phrases	Admire their intellect with "You are very knowledgeable" and "That story was very interesting and informative."
Places for a date	Traditional places such as brand-name shops with status or historic sites such as monuments.
Great gift ideas	A fine, high-quality gift will touch their heart. A traditional gift from an established shop is also a good choice.
Communication	Let them talk about their background and achievements. Be sure to listen carefully.
Caution: Taboos	They get angry when achievements of the past are not respected. Obvious flattery is not good.

You appear plain and sincere, with a modest manner and gentle tone of voice; you always adjust yourself to whom you are talking. Also, you don't like flattery and lies. Since you have strong self-control, you might be taken as weak-spirited and shy. But, in fact, you are very cautious and intelligent, always calculating attentively in your mind who will be beneficial for you. But essentially, you are a warmhearted person full of a volunteering spirit, and you also take good care of your subordinates and people in weak positions. You fear being alone and feel relaxed when you are with lots of people. You can enrich yourself by being in group settings. Having big dreams for the future, you may endure many trials and can steadily make your dreams come true by putting into practice what you have learned from various experiences.

SUCCESS & LUCK: Your Rhythm of Fortune

Know the best time to plan for finance, career, love and more.

❿ Perfection: You will be successful in everything

❾ Success: Your best time for finance and competition

❽ Investment: A good time for networking and money

❼ Change: The right time to start something new

❻ Learning: A time for studies and test-taking

❺ Action: Make your move while in good health

❹ Balance: Organize for harmony

❸ Arrangement: Clean up the clutter in your life

❷ Waste: You tend to waste your time, energy and money

❶ Caution: Be careful in every way, especially when you are communicating with others

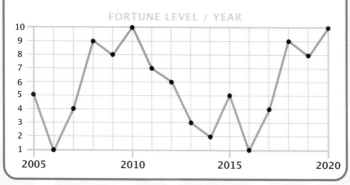

FORTUNE LEVEL / YEAR

A genius at showing consideration for others and never complains

Intelligent and learns a lot from experiences

Famous Sociable Tanukis:

Bill Clinton 8/19/1946
Madonna. 8/16/1958
Christina Aguilera 12/18/1980

8 Glorious TANUKI

You are friendly and genial. Even when you experience something unpleasant, you do not show it in your facial expression. With your gentle smile, you will be loved by your superiors. Having keen eyes for observing people, you can even see through lies and secrets. You value tradition and order and cherish the things of the "good old days." Although you have a mild air, you possess high self-esteem and a somewhat furious temper, as well as clear likes and dislikes. You always stick to a secondary ranking, rather than taking the lead. You cannot be satisfied unless you turn your dreams and thoughts into reality. While you are weak on organizing, you are well suited for outgoing work such as sales or outdoor activities. Having a strong will and clear plans for the future, you can continuously make efforts toward your goal.

SUCCESS & LUCK: Your Rhythm of Fortune

Know the best time to plan for finance, career, love and more.

⑩ Perfection: You will be successful in everything

⑨ Success: Your best time for finance and competition

⑧ Investment: A good time for networking and money

❼ Change: The right time to start something new

❻ Learning: A time for studies and test-taking

❺ Action: Make your move while in good health

❹ Balance: Organize for harmony

❸ Arrangement: Clean up the clutter in your life

❷ Waste: You tend to waste your time, energy and money

❶ Caution: Be careful in every way, especially when you are communicating with others

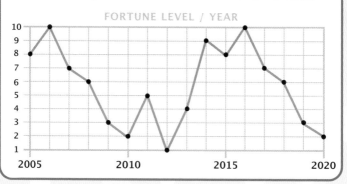

FORTUNE LEVEL / YEAR

♂ Persistent and works hard with all of his ability

♀ Gentle, with gracefulness in her eyes

Famous Glorious Tanukis:

Michelangelo 3/6/1475

John F. Kennedy 5/29/1917

Michelle Pfeiffer 4/29/1957

You are genial and rather passive in attitude, with a warm and gentle personality that is loved by everyone. Since you listen to others very carefully and respond to their expectations, you sometimes control your feelings too much, and this can exhaust you. By nature, you hate restraints and like to have your own way. You are not argumentative but very practical in valuing experiences. Whether it's good or not, lack of adherence is part of your character. You do not cling to the past and always make your way facing forward. You can do good, supportive work under a leader, without expecting any credit. With your calm, philosophical attitude regardless of ambition, and your careful consideration and respect for others, you will be held in high esteem by your superiors and can climb to a higher position. You may one day be the "power behind the throne."

SUCCESS & LUCK: Your Rhythm of Fortune

Know the best time to plan for finance, career, love and more.

🔟 **Perfection:** You will be successful in everything

9️⃣ **Success:** Your best time for finance and competition

8️⃣ **Investment:** A good time for networking and money

7️⃣ **Change:** The right time to start something new

6️⃣ **Learning:** A time for studies and test-taking

5️⃣ **Action:** Make your move while in good health

4️⃣ **Balance:** Organize for harmony

3️⃣ **Arrangement:** Clean up the clutter in your life

2️⃣ **Waste:** You tend to waste your time, energy and money

1️⃣ **Caution:** Be careful in every way, especially when you are communicating with others

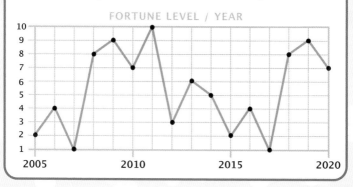

FORTUNE LEVEL / YEAR

 Very strong and can endure a hard life

 Modest and reliable, with great inner strength

Famous Potential Tanukis:

Cyndi Lauper. 6/22/1953

James Cameron. 8/16/1954

Tobey Maguire. 6/27/1975

115

A peacemaker, you are good at mediation. You soften the atmosphere and alleviate the stress between people. Since you tend to resign yourself to a situation, you accept anything as it is. As a result, you sometimes seem as if you have given up or have no interest in the situation. But you have a fighting spirit, and once you aim at your target, you show great concentration in pushing through in spite of hardships. Polite, sincere, diligent and patient, you are a role model of these traits. You can handle things accurately, making prompt decisions and taking action quickly. Having keen eyes for observing people, you manage to make your way through the world. If you work in a group of people, you will be a favorite among the superiors. Since you have the ability to reflect the opinion of the minority, you will be respected and adored by many.

SUCCESS & LUCK: Your Rhythm of Fortune

Know the best time to plan for finance, career, love and more.

❿ Perfection: You will be successful in everything

❾ Success: Your best time for finance and competition

❽ Investment: A good time for networking and money

❼ Change: The right time to start something new

❻ Learning: A time for studies and test-taking

❺ Action: Make your move while in good health

❹ Balance: Organize for harmony

❸ Arrangement: Clean up the clutter in your life

❷ Waste: You tend to waste your time, energy and money

❶ Caution: Be careful in every way, especially when you are communicating with others

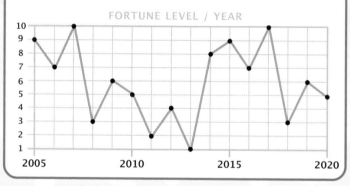

FORTUNE LEVEL / YEAR

 Heartwarming and works for the public good

 Sociable, with a pleasant character

Famous Mighty-Hearted Tanukis:

Julie Andrews 10/1/1935
Cindy Crawford 2/20/1966
Tiger Woods 12/30/1975

KOALA

- like to have time to relax with a still mind

- a romantic with a rich imagination

- like southern islands and hot springs

- full of a helpful and entertaining spirit

- like to take naps and stay up late at night

- never compete unless you are sure to win

- consider things with a long-term perspective

4 **Swift** Koala

10 **Merciful** Koala

16 **King** Koala

33 **Active** Koala

39 **Romantic** Koala

45 **Helpful** Koala

CHARACTER RELATIONSHIPS

Percentage shows how easily a Koala communicates with:

Easy Communication

LION		100%
TIGER		90%
CHEETAH		85%

MONKEY		75%
ELEPHANT		70%
KOALA		60%

Stressful

FAWN		5%
SHEEP		15%
BLACK PANTHER		25%

TANUKI		35%
WOLF		45%
PEGASUS		55%

TIPS & TABOOS: Understanding a Koala

Words & phrases — Express to them with admiration, "I'd love to hear your hopes and dreams" and "That sounds enjoyable."

Places for a date — Relaxing places such as spas and facilities for health and recreation.

Great gift ideas — Tea and health foods. They enjoy gifts that are unaffected by changes in fashion.

Communication — Talk about their future dreams. Listen without making remarks about reality.

Caution: Taboos — Never rush them while they are relaxing. They also hate to hear loud voices.

4 Swift
KOALA

You have a strong will to reach for your dreams with long-term perspective. Although bright and uncomplicated, you are somewhat of a nervous skeptic. You are restless as well as short-tempered and impatient. But you feel stressed unless you give yourself enough time to feel at ease and relaxed. Although sociable and able to communicate with lots of people, you open your heart only to those who are really cordial with you. But since you have keen, observant eyes, you are successful in choosing friends. You are very tight with money and do not waste or buy impulsively. You can tend to be too absorbed in your interests and might indulge in your imaginary world. Be careful not to lose your social skills and keep yourself well balanced.

SUCCESS & LUCK: Your Rhythm of Fortune

Know the best time to plan for finance, career, love and more.

❿ Perfection: You will be successful in everything

❾ Success: Your best time for finance and competition

❽ Investment: A good time for networking and money

❼ Change: The right time to start something new

❻ Learning: A time for studies and test-taking

❺ Action: Make your move while in good health

❹ Balance: Organize for harmony

❸ Arrangement: Clean up the clutter in your life

❷ Waste: You tend to waste your time, energy and money

❶ Caution: Be careful in every way, especially when you are communicating with others

FORTUNE LEVEL / YEAR

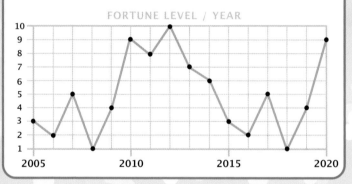

 Bright, active and sociable

 Romantic dreamer who is very cautious

Famous Swift Koalas:

Stanley Kubrick. 7/26/1928

Harrison Ford 7/13/1942

Emma Thompson 4/15/1959

10 Merciful KOALA

Y ou are a considerate and caring person but have high self-esteem and are somewhat of a skeptic. Since you have a natural, frank attitude, you are very reliable. But if someone hurts your pride, you can really get angry. Since you have both sides to your character, the difference between your good and bad moods is very obvious. If you run into difficulty, you react with an intensity that is unimaginable, given your gentle appearance. You are rather conservative in your ideas and try to figure out what action to take in the present moment. Although you act quickly and are smooth in handling situations, if you jump the gun, you may get into useless conflicts and make things even more complicated. If you can find someone who will give you good advice, your innate fortune to shine and succeed in life will open up.

SUCCESS & LUCK: Your Rhythm of Fortune

Know the best time to plan for finance, career, love and more.

⑩ Perfection: You will be successful in everything

⑨ Success: Your best time for finance and competition

⑧ Investment: A good time for networking and money

⑦ Change: The right time to start something new

⑥ Learning: A time for studies and test-taking

⑤ Action: Make your move while in good health

④ Balance: Organize for harmony

③ Arrangement: Clean up the clutter in your life

② Waste: You tend to waste your time, energy and money

① Caution: Be careful in every way, especially when you are communicating with others

FORTUNE LEVEL / YEAR

Likes to take care of others but needs to be cared for

Smart and skilled at making her way in life

Famous Merciful Koalas:

Thomas Jefferson 4/13/1743

Hideo Nomo 8/31/1968

Alanis Morissette 6/1/1974

123

You believe you are the one who will laugh last, even if you are having difficulty now. With strong likes and dislikes, you will sacrifice your needs to take care of the person you favor, but you close your eyes to whom you don't. You have enemies as well as friends. If you become more tolerant, you will always find yourself under a lucky star. Because of your spark of genius, you often change your mind. On the other hand, you are very deliberate in making steady efforts. You are shy but optimistic. Having keen intuition, you understand things quickly and are very good at making your point understood. Since you are argumentative, you never accept unreasonable situations or something that you cannot consent to. You are tight with money, so you will not have monetary hardships. You value action more than words, and being strong enough to bear intense discipline, you know how to succeed in life.

SUCCESS & LUCK: Your Rhythm of Fortune

Know the best time to plan for finance, career, love and more.

10 Perfection: You will be successful in everything

9 Success: Your best time for finance and competition

8 Investment: A good time for networking and money

7 Change: The right time to start something new

6 Learning: A time for studies and test-taking

5 Action: Make your move while in good health

4 Balance: Organize for harmony

3 Arrangement: Clean up the clutter in your life

2 Waste: You tend to waste your time, energy and money

1 Caution: Be careful in every way, especially when you are communicating with others

FORTUNE LEVEL / YEAR

♂ Has a rich imagination and keen inspiration

♀ Ambitious, with motherly tendencies

Famous King Koalas:

Jack Nicholson. 4/22/1937
Kevin Costner. 1/18/1955
Uma Thurman. 4/29/1970

125

Although you pretend to be simple and casual, inwardly you are sensitive and delicate. Having political skill and power, you always aim for the top. You are warmhearted and easily moved to tears, and you can even become addicted to the sentiments of others, as well as your own. But on the other hand, beware that there are times when you pay no attention to the less fortunate because of your private profit or judge people only by their ability. You are excitable but quick to cool down, and you have a strong sense for social movement and the ability to be ahead of the times. You treasure the spirit of romantic adventure in life, but you do not lose your sense of reality. Since you have these opposing characteristics, people think that you are not easy to understand. The courage to express your character will lead you to success. If you find a superior who understands you well, you will be all the more successful.

SUCCESS & LUCK: Your Rhythm of Fortune

Know the best time to plan for finance, career, love and more.

10 Perfection: You will be successful in everything

9 Success: Your best time for finance and competition

8 Investment: A good time for networking and money

7 Change: The right time to start something new

6 Learning: A time for studies and test-taking

5 Action: Make your move while in good health

4 Balance: Organize for harmony

3 Arrangement: Clean up the clutter in your life

2 Waste: You tend to waste your time, energy and money

1 Caution: Be careful in every way, especially when you are communicating with others

FORTUNE LEVEL / YEAR

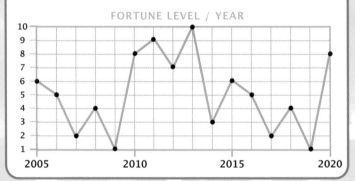

♂ Has the skills to live his own life

♀ Hardworking, with a rich imagination

Famous Active Koalas:

Nelson Mandela 7/18/1918

Yogi Berra 5/12/1925

Charlotte Church 2/21/1986

You are frank and natural, and also very sociable and adaptable. Since you hate to be alone, you are always surrounded by friends. You can quickly discern the essence of things and are also skilled at managing people. Being well aware of your short temper and impulsive character, you always restrain yourself. Although generous with others, you become quite emotional about yourself and can sometimes be selfish. You are a sensible person and a unique character with original ideas. You like to live in a world full of variety and try to make changes in your life and surrounding circumstances. You have the power to make your romantic dreams come true, but sometimes you get too unrealistic. If you show your ability in learning environments, or in business as a leader or coach, you will be blessed with great success.

SUCCESS & LUCK: Your Rhythm of Fortune

Know the best time to plan for finance, career, love and more.

10 Perfection: You will be successful in everything

9 Success: Your best time for finance and competition

8 Investment: A good time for networking and money

7 Change: The right time to start something new

6 Learning: A time for studies and test-taking

5 Action: Make your move while in good health

4 Balance: Organize for harmony

3 Arrangement: Clean up the clutter in your life

2 Waste: You tend to waste your time, energy and money

1 Caution: Be careful in every way, especially when you are communicating with others

FORTUNE LEVEL / YEAR

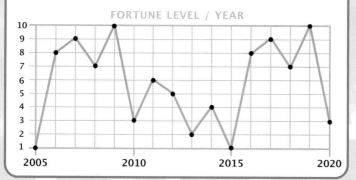

♂ Makes steady efforts for the future

♀ Very popular, with keen intuition

Famous Romantic Koalas:

Ludwig van Beethoven. 12/16/1770

Paul McCartney. 6/18/1942

Tom Cruise. 7/3/1962

You are elegant, intelligent and very friendly, and these traits are respected by others. You avoid quarrels and like to have well-rounded relations, so you tend to be cautious in expressing yourself. Since you keep everyone at the same distance, you will be taken as "everyone's friend." But you hate to go along with something unreasonable or follow unconditionally the powers that be. You are strict with and faithful to yourself and will not be moved by personal profit. Since you are sensitive, you sometimes show your temperamental side only to your close friends. You are a romantic with a superior artistic sense. Be careful not to be self-satisfying; try to see things objectively. Since you are quick-witted and have strong intuition, you will manage to do well and succeed in any line of work. Your truthfulness in working toward any position will be highly esteemed.

SUCCESS & LUCK: Your Rhythm of Fortune

Know the best time to plan for finance, career, love and more.

⑩ Perfection: You will be successful in everything

⑨ Success: Your best time for finance and competition

⑧ Investment: A good time for networking and money

❼ Change: The right time to start something new

❻ Learning: A time for studies and test-taking

❺ Action: Make your move while in good health

❹ Balance: Organize for harmony

❸ Arrangement: Clean up the clutter in your life

❷ Waste: You tend to waste your time, energy and money

❶ Caution: Be careful in every way, especially when you are communicating with others

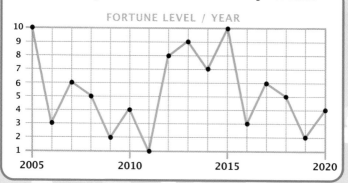

FORTUNE LEVEL / YEAR

 Has a fighting spirit to maintain peace

♀ Intelligent and good at handling complaints

Famous Helpful Koalas:

Lucille Ball 8/6/1911
Mickey Mantle 10/20/1931
Stevie Wonder 5/13/1950

ELEPHANT

- always devoted to something

- a person of efforts and perseverance

- often talk big

- hate to be kept waiting

- have an ear for gossip but sometimes don't listen attentively

- clearly distinguish friends from enemies

- out of control once temper is lost

· ·

12 **Popular** Elephant

18 **Delicate** Elephant

31 **Chief** Elephant

37 **Rushing** Elephant

CHARACTER RELATIONSHIPS

Percentage shows how easily an Elephant communicates with:

Easy Communication				Stressful			
TANUKI	🌙	✊	100%	WOLF	🌑	✌	5%
LION	☀	✋	90%	KOALA	🌑	✌	15%
BLACK PANTHER	⬤	✊	85%	MONKEY	🌑	✌	25%

⬇

CHEETAH	☀	✋	75%	TIGER	🌑	✌	35%
SHEEP	⬤	✊	70%	PEGASUS	☀	✋	45%
ELEPHANT	☀	✋	60%	FAWN	🌙	✊	55%

⬆ ➡

TIPS & TABOOS: Understanding an Elephant

Words & phrases — Praise them with "You're great!" and "You put your heart and soul into that."

Places for a date — Large shops and places with beautiful landscapes and panoramic views. They don't enjoy going to small places.

Great gift ideas — Something touted by celebrities. Globes and picture books are also good choices.

Communication — Whatever the topic may be, it's important to listen to them very carefully.

Caution: Taboos — The phrase "Aren't you listening to me?" is taboo. Being late for an occasion is definitely not good.

Since you are a bit stubborn, you might feel uneasy while communicating with others. You don't depend on people and hate restraints, so you prefer more distant relations and avoid being too close to others. Always calm, you keep a steady mind without being influenced by your surroundings. Aggressive and active without any shyness, you are respected as a big brother/sister type. You love to have fun, but you put work before all else. Your motto is: "Don't put off until tomorrow what you can do today," and having the pride of a professional, you don't mind staying up all night to work. You are a perfectionist who hates to compromise. When you feel uncertain or insecure, you give up quickly and start something new. Be careful that if you overestimate yourself, you might shut your ears to others' opinions and lose your self-control. To avoid misunderstandings with friends, try to understand their feelings.

SUCCESS & LUCK: Your Rhythm of Fortune

Know the best time to plan for finance, career, love and more.

⑩ Perfection: You will be successful in everything

⑨ Success: Your best time for finance and competition

⑧ Investment: A good time for networking and money

❼ Change: The right time to start something new

❻ Learning: A time for studies and test-taking

❺ Action: Make your move while in good health

❹ Balance: Organize for harmony

❸ Arrangement: Clean up the clutter in your life

❷ Waste: You tend to waste your time, energy and money

❶ Caution: Be careful in every way, especially when you are communicating with others

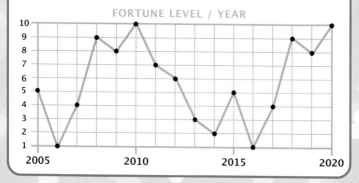

FORTUNE LEVEL / YEAR

♂ Friendly and attention-loving

♀ Proficient in something and knows how to make her way in life

Famous Popular Elephants:

Auguste Rodin. 11/12/1840

John Wayne 5/26/1907

Bridget Fonda 1/27/1964

18 Delicate ELEPHANT

You are calm, self-possessed and have a dignified appearance. Your resolute attitude shows your grace. With "efforts and guts" as your motto, your character is pure and sincere by nature. You maintain frank relations with others and do not read between the lines. Having keen eyes on your interests, you value actual profit and efficiency. You will choose something interesting and useful for your pastime. You study hard and work hard, making steady efforts while no one notices, and you achieve good results consistently. You have an ear for rumors and private discussion, but beware that you sometimes do not listen attentively to the person whom you are talking with. You have high self-esteem, as well as strict morals and a short temper. Both mature and childish sides are evident in your character, and this imbalance is your charm.

SUCCESS & LUCK: Your Rhythm of Fortune

Know the best time to plan for finance, career, love and more.

⑩ Perfection: You will be successful in everything

⑨ Success: Your best time for finance and competition

⑧ Investment: A good time for networking and money

⑦ Change: The right time to start something new

⑥ Learning: A time for studies and test-taking

⑤ Action: Make your move while in good health

④ Balance: Organize for harmony

③ Arrangement: Clean up the clutter in your life

② Waste: You tend to waste your time, energy and money

① Caution: Be careful in every way, especially when you are communicating with others

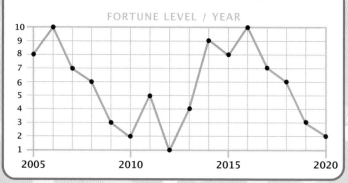

FORTUNE LEVEL / YEAR

 Able to judge what is right and wrong

Dainty and pretty, with an attractive air

Famous Delicate Elephants:

George Frederic Handel..... 2/23/1685

Clint Eastwood 5/31/1930

Angelina Jolie 6/4/1975

You are a diamond in the rough and very dynamic. Since you are honest, single-minded and friendly, you make a good impression on others. You can communicate with all people and maintain well-rounded relations. You value effort above all else and hate laziness, and you never cut corners or compromise in business. Since you hold others to the same principles, you tend to be very strict with those who are irresponsible, and they might feel uncomfortable. Be broad-minded and keep in mind that somebody else's business is not necessarily your own. As you don't complain or whine, you will be terribly shocked when you meet with failure. You have strong enough willpower to specialize and make great achievements in a certain field. But try to be well balanced, and broaden your focus. You need time to be understood by others, but you will succeed in gaining respect from many people in the long run.

SUCCESS & LUCK: Your Rhythm of Fortune

Know the best time to plan for finance, career, love and more.

10 Perfection: You will be successful in everything

9 Success: Your best time for finance and competition

8 Investment: A good time for networking and money

7 Change: The right time to start something new

6 Learning: A time for studies and test-taking

5 Action: Make your move while in good health

4 Balance: Organize for harmony

3 Arrangement: Clean up the clutter in your life

2 Waste: You tend to waste your time, energy and money

1 Caution: Be careful in every way, especially when you are communicating with others

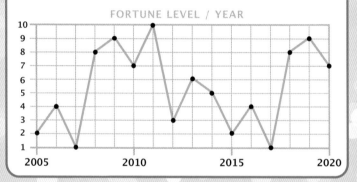

FORTUNE LEVEL / YEAR

♂ Has willpower, perseverance and guts

♀ Pure, with a giving spirit

Famous Chief Elephants:

Napoleon Bonaparte 8/15/1769

James Dean 2/8/1931

Sophia Loren. 9/20/1934

Y ou are polite, elegant and gentle. Although you are attractive, you don't play up to the opposite sex, so you are admired by the same sex, as well. Gutsy and patient, you are stable and are not disturbed by small matters. But since you have a quiet and delicate side, you notice every detail and are quite considerate in caring for others. You don't get too discouraged even when you fail, and you can change your mind quickly. You give an honest, unselfish impression. Although you have the ability to pick up on the trends of the world, you don't have the political savvy to pull strings. So you are better at working as an individual rather than a leader of a group. You will be trusted for your efforts in seeking a goal and for always keeping your promises. You might show your selfishness openly with your family, but never to others.

SUCCESS & LUCK: Your Rhythm of Fortune

Know the best time to plan for finance, career, love and more.

10 Perfection: You will be successful in everything

9 Success: Your best time for finance and competition

8 Investment: A good time for networking and money

7 Change: The right time to start something new

6 Learning: A time for studies and test-taking

5 Action: Make your move while in good health

4 Balance: Organize for harmony

3 Arrangement: Clean up the clutter in your life

2 Waste: You tend to waste your time, energy and money

1 Caution: Be careful in every way, especially when you are communicating with others

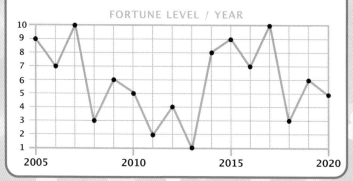

FORTUNE LEVEL / YEAR

♂ Open-hearted and forges headlong toward a goal

♀ Active, with an independent mind

Famous Rushing Elephants:

Henry Kissinger 5/27/1923

Bill Cosby. 7/12/1937

Jennifer Lopez 7/24/1969

SHEEP

- feel lonely often and hate to be alone
- don't want to be excluded from the group
- enjoy gathering varied information (a good researcher)

- value harmony
- like to save money
- struggle with saying no when invited somewhere
- tend to complain and grumble

14 **Solitary** Sheep

20 **Harmonious** Sheep

23 **Innocent** Sheep

26 **Humane** Sheep

29 **Adventurous** Sheep

35 **Reliable** Sheep

CHARACTER RELATIONSHIPS

Percentage shows how easily a Sheep communicates with:

Easy Communication

TIGER			100%
TANUKI			90%
MONKEY			85%

BLACK PANTHER			75%
KOALA			70%
SHEEP			60%

Stressful

PEGASUS			5%
ELEPHANT			15%
CHEETAH			25%

LION			35%
FAWN			45%
WOLF			55%

TIPS & TABOOS: Understanding a Sheep

Words & phrases
Communicate with consideration, "I see," "I understand you" and "I agree."

Places for a date
Places and shops where lovers can walk hand in hand.

Great gift ideas
Collectable gifts. They also enjoy receiving postcards from those traveling abroad.

Communication
They have lots of information and like to discuss rumors. They will be delighted if you listened admiringly.

Caution: Taboos
Being left out of the group is a stressful situation for them. Having a private, confidential talk is taboo.

Y ou have a calm, composed air and never show off, and you live your life slowly and steadily. You can be quite considerate in communicating with others, but in spite of your modest impression you have high self-esteem, so you refuse to do anything that is forced upon you. You do not waver in your opinions, and you are skilled at sticking to your demands. You have clear ideals and always hope for a higher level than your present circumstances. You do not hold prejudices in your thoughts or in your relations with others, and you enjoy offering your counsel and giving advice. But you, too, have complaints and often grumble. You sometimes get angry and cool down without expressing your thoughts and can be taken as a suggestive person by the opposite sex. You lack aggressiveness, but by using your ability to discern others' thoughts and judge objectively, you can be successful.

SUCCESS & LUCK: Your Rhythm of Fortune

Know the best time to plan for finance, career, love and more.

⑩ Perfection: You will be successful in everything

⑨ Success: Your best time for finance and competition

⑧ Investment: A good time for networking and money

⑦ Change: The right time to start something new

⑥ Learning: A time for studies and test-taking

⑤ Action: Make your move while in good health

④ Balance: Organize for harmony

③ Arrangement: Clean up the clutter in your life

② Waste: You tend to waste your time, energy and money

① Caution: Be careful in every way, especially when you are communicating with others

FORTUNE LEVEL / YEAR

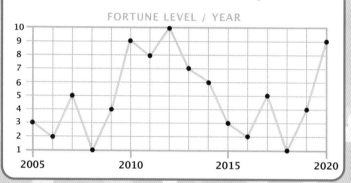

♂ Doesn't follow the flock like other sheep

♀ Good-natured and lives within her means

Famous Solitary Sheep:

Thomas Edison 2/11/1847
Federico Fellini 1/20/1920
Tom Hanks 7/9/1956

You do not challenge people's opinions and take safe, steady steps in life. Calm and cool, you make decisions and put them into practice objectively—you are not adventurous. You have high ideals, and your expectations of others tend to be too high. A scholar rather than an athlete, you have a rich imagination and great knowledge. You know the inner workings of the world and keep up on social movements. Since you love to work for humanity and the world and never pander to authority, you have the abilities of a reformer. Though gentle in attitude, you have a strong sense of self, and once you assert yourself, you can be stubborn and will not give up easily. Try to be more flexible. You also have a moody side and quickly change what you say according to your feelings. Although you believe communication is important, you like to be alone as well, and you recognize this contradiction within yourself.

SUCCESS & LUCK: Your Rhythm of Fortune

Know the best time to plan for finance, career, love and more.

10 Perfection: You will be successful in everything

9 Success: Your best time for finance and competition

8 Investment: A good time for networking and money

7 Change: The right time to start something new

6 Learning: A time for studies and test-taking

5 Action: Make your move while in good health

4 Balance: Organize for harmony

3 Arrangement: Clean up the clutter in your life

2 Waste: You tend to waste your time, energy and money

1 Caution: Be careful in every way, especially when you are communicating with others

FORTUNE LEVEL / YEAR

 Very steady and thinks carefully before moving ahead

 Has a fighting spirit deep inside

Famous Harmonious Sheep:

Meryl Streep 6/22/1949

Johnny Depp. 6/9/1963

Kirsten Dunst 4/30/1982

Y ou give off a somewhat childlike impression. Though you are adaptable and tenderhearted, you often feel lonely and lack an independent mind, preferring to depend on others. Since you are a fast learner, you handle things well and will have a favorable reputation, but you are a shy person at your core. You rarely express yourself because you do not want to show your true character or make yourself stand out. Adaptable to new circumstances, you tend to be influenced by life's changes, so you will experience big ups and downs. But you have a strong mind and the ability to calculate your profits, and you are good at dealing with people. You praise those who are likely to be your friends. Having keen eyes, you are skilled at discerning the most advantageous position. Once you begin something you continue with patience, but sometimes you may fall behind because of your cautiousness.

SUCCESS & LUCK: Your Rhythm of Fortune

Know the best time to plan for finance, career, love and more.

⓵⓪ **Perfection**: You will be successful in everything

⑨ **Success**: Your best time for finance and competition

⑧ **Investment**: A good time for networking and money

⑦ **Change**: The right time to start something new

⑥ **Learning**: A time for studies and test-taking

⑤ **Action**: Make your move while in good health

④ **Balance**: Organize for harmony

③ **Arrangement**: Clean up the clutter in your life

② **Waste**: You tend to waste your time, energy and money

① **Caution**: Be careful in every way, especially when you are communicating with others

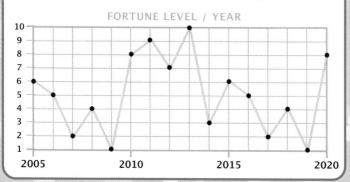

FORTUNE LEVEL / YEAR

Loves freedom and hates to be restrained

Frank and good at caring for others

Famous Innocent Sheep:

Florence Nightingale 5/12/1820
Sharon Stone 3/10/1958
Brandon Lee 2/1/1965

Y ou are soft and modest in attitude and give the impression of being a refined lady/gentleman. A sociable person with a knack for encyclopedic knowledge, you never run out of topics in conversation. Socially, you conduct yourself with sound common sense. You value the spirit of cooperation and do not allow people to disturb the peace. You hate to lose, have self-confidence and work very hard for your likes and interests. Since you gather all kinds of information so that you can keep current, you will not find yourself too absorbed in a certain field. A talented person, you aim for perfection, but you are also flexible and well balanced. Sometimes you can sulk like a child when things do not turn out as you have expected. But you are considerate enough to care for others.

SUCCESS & LUCK: Your Rhythm of Fortune

Know the best time to plan for finance, career, love and more.

⑩ Perfection: You will be successful in everything

⑨ Success: Your best time for finance and competition

⑧ Investment: A good time for networking and money

⑦ Change: The right time to start something new

⑥ Learning: A time for studies and test-taking

⑤ Action: Make your move while in good health

④ Balance: Organize for harmony

③ Arrangement: Clean up the clutter in your life

② Waste: You tend to waste your time, energy and money

① Caution: Be careful in every way, especially when you are communicating with others

FORTUNE LEVEL / YEAR

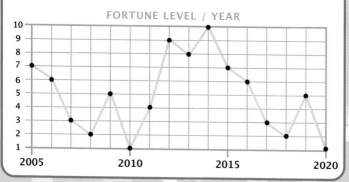

 Has a strong sense of duty and loyalty

♀ Peace-loving with a calm and quiet life

Famous Humane Sheep:

Sigmund Freud 5/6/1856

Larry King 11/19/1933

Helen Hunt 6/15/1963

Since you are a mild and calm person who gives off a quiet impression, everyone likes you. Very wise and modest, you love the spirit of cooperation. On the contrary, you also sometimes regret undertaking a heavy task without considering it carefully. You try to keep a certain distance with others and do not necessarily express yourself openly. But you are very sensitive to trends and like to attend parties and meetings. You are highly competitive and have the strong will and persistence to reach a goal by yourself. Although you have good luck and are gifted with a keen sense for catching on to new trends, your conclusions tend to be guided by the current times, which makes you slow in decision and action. In terms of finances, you always make economic aspects the top priority and have a clear vision regarding profit and loss.

SUCCESS & LUCK: Your Rhythm of Fortune

Know the best time to plan for finance, career, love and more.

10 Perfection: You will be successful in everything

9 Success: Your best time for finance and competition

8 Investment: A good time for networking and money

7 Change: The right time to start something new

6 Learning: A time for studies and test-taking

5 Action: Make your move while in good health

4 Balance: Organize for harmony

3 Arrangement: Clean up the clutter in your life

2 Waste: You tend to waste your time, energy and money

1 Caution: Be careful in every way, especially when you are communicating with others

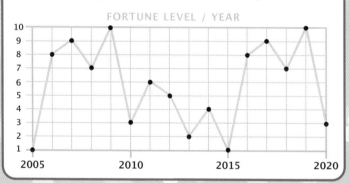

FORTUNE LEVEL / YEAR

σ Business-like, with sound judgment

♀ Cool and intelligent, with an artistic sense

Famous Adventurous Sheep:

Pablo Picasso 10/25/1881
Michael Douglas 9/25/1944
Sissy Spacek 12/25/1949

You are calm and composed in anyone's company and do not waver in your opinions and values. You are faithful and humane with a passion for justice. Having great self-respect, you often think, "I'm the best." You hate to be ordered around or forced into doing something. Skilled at negotiating and praising others, you are a genius at organizing things to achieve a desirable outcome. Though strict in calculating profit and loss, you strive to accept the favor of others and cannot say no when you are relied upon. You are talented at planning and sharing ideas. Without adhering strictly to your ideals, you use your intellect to analyze, and you have the power to carry out ideas that no one could imagine. You tend to be lax on making decisions and seeing prospects when you are too excited, and you might make mistakes. But you have vitality as well as persistence and rarely give up.

SUCCESS & LUCK: Your Rhythm of Fortune

Know the best time to plan for finance, career, love and more.

⑩ Perfection: You will be successful in everything

⑨ Success: Your best time for finance and competition

⑧ Investment: A good time for networking and money

⑦ Change: The right time to start something new

⑥ Learning: A time for studies and test-taking

⑤ Action: Make your move while in good health

④ Balance: Organize for harmony

③ Arrangement: Clean up the clutter in your life

② Waste: You tend to waste your time, energy and money

① Caution: Be careful in every way, especially when you are communicating with others

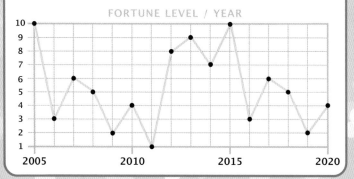

FORTUNE LEVEL / YEAR

 Creative, with a positive mind

 Good at caring for and praising others

Famous Reliable Sheep:

Galileo Galilei 2/15/1564

Will Smith 9/25/1968

Derek Jeter 6/26/1974

155

PEGASUS

- a genius type who gives an otherworldly impression

- have strong intuition and catch on quickly

- hate to be restrained

- have difficulty understanding yourself

- hard to stay in one place; enjoy moving around

- tend to think about something other than the topic at hand

- moody and temperamental

- -

21 **Calm** Pegasus

22 **Flexible** Pegasus

27 **Dramatic** Pegasus

28 **Elegant** Pegasus

CHARACTER RELATIONSHIPS

Percentage shows how easily a Pegasus communicates with:

Easy Communication

SHEEP	⬤ ✊	100%
ELEPHANT	☀ ✋	90%
TANUKI	🌙 ✊	85%

⬇

LION	☀ ✋	75%
FAWN	🌙 ✊	70%
PEGASUS	☀ ✋	60%

➡

Stressful

MONKEY	⬤ ✌	5%
WOLF	⬤ ✌	15%
TIGER	⬤ ✌	25%

⬆

KOALA	⬤ ✌	35%
CHEETAH	☀ ✋	45%
BLACK PANTHER	⬤ ✊	55%

TIPS & TABOOS: Understanding a Pegasus

Words & phrases Praise with openness, "That sounds nice" and "I admire your being so free."

Places for a date Best places to visit will depend on their mood. Strict plans are stressful.

Great gift ideas Presents with an otherworldly feel. Gifts with an angel motif or an image of the universe are good choices.

Communication They often change the topic, but this is unimportant. Listen with a light air.

Caution: Taboos Restraints and commands are not good. They hate to hear about common sense and do not make decisions based on the majority's opinion.

You appear gentle and moderate, with a refined sense of fashion. You are charming and friendly, easily moved by silly stories, and you often use over-exaggerated expressions to show your feelings. Although sociable, inwardly you are very sensitive and cautious. So you consciously pretend to be genial in order to hide your true feelings. You have strong likes and dislikes about people, as well as food, but once you believe somebody, it is very firm. You can be somewhat coquettish and easily flattered. Since you love freedom of thought and hate restraints, you are well suited for individual rather than group work. Full of curiosity, you are very sensitive to social movements. You always depend on your inspiration, mood and sensibilities, and so you tend to be rather unsteady and flighty. But when you get highly motivated, you can show an unbelievable power and have the potential to earn a lot of money.

SUCCESS & LUCK: Your Rhythm of Fortune

Know the best time to plan for finance, career, love and more.

⑩ Perfection: You will be successful in everything

⑨ Success: Your best time for finance and competition

⑧ Investment: A good time for networking and money

❼ Change: The right time to start something new

❻ Learning: A time for studies and test-taking

❺ Action: Make your move while in good health

❹ Balance: Organize for harmony

❸ Arrangement: Clean up the clutter in your life

❷ Waste: You tend to waste your time, energy and money

❶ Caution: Be careful in every way, especially when you are communicating with others

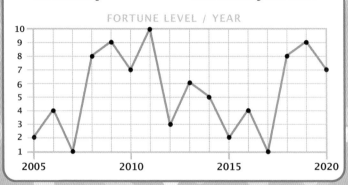

FORTUNE LEVEL / YEAR

 Has great ideas and outstanding abilities

♀ Idealistic and full of vitality

Famous Calm Pegasus:

Carl Sagan 11/9/1934
Jimi Hendrix 11/27/1942
Whitney Houston 8/9/1963

22 Flexible
PEGASUS

Since you have a wild air and dignified attitude, your impression is somewhat proud and unapproachable. But in fact, you are frank and friendly to the people you can trust. You have the passion to chase your ideals, but since you don't like to make waves, you handle things with a flexible attitude according to the circumstances. You also have keen, discerning eyes. Having a wide pool of acquaintances and connections in many fields, you have the ability to become a leader who is careful and considerate. But your ideal is to live without restraints, so you are strong in individual work rather than teamwork. Your weak point is following instructions tightly and promptly. Since you value the process of work, you handle things with the closest attention until completion, but after it's done, you quickly lose interest in it.

SUCCESS & LUCK: Your Rhythm of Fortune

Know the best time to plan for finance, career, love and more.

10 Perfection: You will be successful in everything

9 Success: Your best time for finance and competition

8 Investment: A good time for networking and money

7 Change: The right time to start something new

6 Learning: A time for studies and test-taking

5 Action: Make your move while in good health

4 Balance: Organize for harmony

3 Arrangement: Clean up the clutter in your life

2 Waste: You tend to waste your time, energy and money

1 Caution: Be careful in every way, especially when you are communicating with others

FORTUNE LEVEL / YEAR

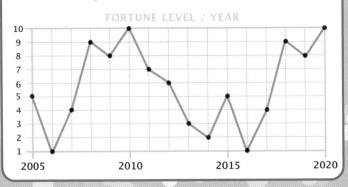

♂ Has a strong character and is friendly to all

♀ Very active and often rushes headlong into something

Famous Flexible Pegasus:

George Washington 2/22/1732

John Lennon 10/9/1940

Oprah Winfrey. 1/29/1954

You have a mysterious air and appear unapproachable, yet you are friendly. You have a somewhat dramatic character with much sensibility and imagination. Generally, you are cheerful, active and frank, but sometimes you get moody and experience emotional ups and downs. Sensitive and lacking endurance, you often change your plans or have difficulty in continuing with a repetitive task, but you rarely fail in your communication. Since you are considerate, you behave generously with a sense of purpose. You can analyze thoroughly, have the intuition to see through people and have foresight, but you tend to be weak in the final stages and sometimes fail to succeed in spite of your effort. Make the most of your broad knowledge and inspiration to show your wonderful abilities; otherwise, you may find that you've wandered away from your goals without knowing your purpose in life.

SUCCESS & LUCK: Your Rhythm of Fortune

Know the best time to plan for finance, career, love and more.

⑩ Perfection: You will be successful in everything

⑨ Success: Your best time for finance and competition

⑧ Investment: A good time for networking and money

⑦ Change: The right time to start something new

⑥ Learning: A time for studies and test-taking

⑤ Action: Make your move while in good health

④ Balance: Organize for harmony

③ Arrangement: Clean up the clutter in your life

② Waste: You tend to waste your time, energy and money

① Caution: Be careful in every way, especially when you are communicating with others

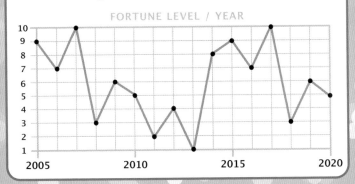

FORTUNE LEVEL / YEAR

 Moody and has rich emotions

 A traveler with big ups and downs

Famous Dramatic Pegasus:

Henry Ford 7/30/1863
Ethan Hawke. 11/6/1970
Shakira. 2/2/1977

163

Single-minded and hating unfairness, you have a straight-forward character. Tenderhearted and easily moved with sympathy for others, you may become burdened with other people's troubles. You are not skilled at dealing with people, and this awkwardness makes you all the more charming. Having a strong sense of responsibility and for chasing after your ideals, you are somewhat stubborn in your opinions and can offer cool retorts to your enemies. But you lack consistency in your attitude and are also weak in endurance. Since you are gifted with adaptability, capability and the power to take quick action, you will gain respect from many people and may become a leader without intending to do so. You aim at your goal with the brightness and strength to overcome difficulties, but when you run into problems and come to a standstill, you sometimes grow desperate. Try to stay calm and composed.

SUCCESS & LUCK: Your Rhythm of Fortune

Know the best time to plan for finance, career, love and more.

10 **Perfection**: You will be successful in everything

9 **Success**: Your best time for finance and competition

8 **Investment**: A good time for networking and money

7 **Change**: The right time to start something new

6 **Learning**: A time for studies and test-taking

5 **Action**: Make your move while in good health

4 **Balance**: Organize for harmony

3 **Arrangement**: Clean up the clutter in your life

2 **Waste**: You tend to waste your time, energy and money

1 **Caution**: Be careful in every way, especially when you are communicating with others

FORTUNE LEVEL / YEAR

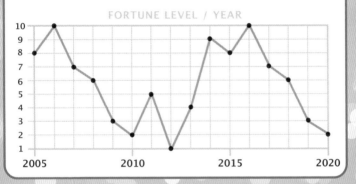

♂ Warmhearted, caring and enjoys beautiful things

♀ Charming and friendly, with first-class taste

Famous Elegant Pegasus:

Marie Curie 11/7/1867
Peter Fonda 2/23/1939
Michael Jordan 2/17/1963

Conversations

Locate your character below, and find out what first impressions you typically make on others, as well as how to improve your conversation skills for better communication.

 WOLF: You look unapproachable because you are a person of few words, but you don't necessarily have to force yourself to be friendly. If you turn your attention to others' strengths and praise them with a few words, the mood will soften.

 FAWN: If you feign cuteness and give off a goody-goody impression, the same sex will feel hostility toward you. At the beginning of a conversation, you tend to talk about rumors. Instead, try to choose topics that attract the interest of the person you are talking with.

 MONKEY: You are at ease with everyone. Since you are competitive, you want to hold the dominant position in conversation, but try to accept others first. You will make a better impression if you consider the position or standpoint of others.

 CHEETAH: You show your likes and dislikes too strongly right from the start. Also, you can tend to be kind to the opposite sex but rather unfriendly to the same sex. In order to avoid making enemies for no reason, try to make congenial small talk with everyone.

 BLACK PANTHER: Your keen eyes for assessing others' fashion sense can make people nervous. Try to chat about light topics (e.g., favorite TV shows), and create a friendly atmosphere. It is best to purposely steer away from topics of fashion and style.

 LION: Your attitude toward others differs greatly according to their appearance or occupation, so try to be more impartial toward everyone. Do not ask direct questions right at the beginning, but start with lighter conversation instead.

TIGER: You tend to speak straightforwardly, even from the first introduction, and may sometimes hurt others' feelings. Above all, it is not good to deny someone's opinion and assert yours. Try to listen first, and your impression will be much better.

 TANUKI: You always have a smile on your face, but since it is difficult to read your real intentions, others might feel a sense of uneasiness. Try to open yourself up in the conversation with phrases like "To tell you the truth . . ."

 KOALA: Your manner and impression can differ depending on your health condition and mood. So try to be in as good a condition as possible to give a pleasant first impression. Since you tend to show your doubt through questions, making gentle conversation would be better.

 ELEPHANT: You often care too much about time, or sometimes do not listen to the conversation and give an unpleasant impression to others. Try to listen attentively, even if the topic might not be very interesting to you. Having a friendly air is the most important thing when you meet someone for the first time.

 SHEEP: Because you fear being left out of conversations, you tend to talk too much about yourself and give an impression of self-satisfaction. When you talk, try to show consideration for others by using phrases such as "What do you think?" or "How about you?" and then let others answer.

 PEGASUS: You give off a moody and otherworldly impression. Your conversation can tend to be rambling, and others might find it difficult to keep up. Although it may be bothersome, try to make your meaning more understandable.

Business Settings

Locate your character below to learn about your personality, impression and work habits in business settings.

 WOLF: You are a businesslike person who is much relied upon by others. But you are not very friendly or sociable. Though you tend to be impatient when you undertake more than one task, if you organize them in order of priority, you will work efficiently.

 FAWN: You work enthusiastically when you are praised or being counted on. But when deadlines get close, you feel stress and tend to become desperate. The trick of completing daily tasks is to work constantly and steadily, even if it may seem very simple and tiresome.

 MONKEY: You are a quick worker and excellent at handling things. But check your work thoroughly, since you tend to draw hasty conclusions. Be careful about flattering your superiors, which can sometimes end up putting you in a tight corner.

 CHEETAH: You only speed up the pace of your work when going into the last stage. Even if you don't mind this, your coworkers will worry about it. When working in a team, it is important to report the process of your work.

 BLACK PANTHER: You are good at gathering information and making plans. Be sure to share information with others. You tend to care too much about your reputation in the office, but if you work hard you will surely be respected.

 LION: Since you always aim for perfection and hate to show your weaknesses to others, you tend to keep your mistakes to yourself. Go to your seniors for advice and you will resolve problems much more quickly. Don't be obstinate.

TIGER: You are a wise worker with a sense of balance, which allows you to do your work with the overall perspective in mind. Relied on by both your seniors and juniors, your only fault is losing your temper when your working pace is disturbed by someone.

 TANUKI: You tend to take on too much work and get into a panic. It should be a rule for you to refuse work you cannot handle. You are treasured by others, as you often help to reduce friction in your office.

 KOALA: Since you tend to be a slow starter, it is hard to adjust your pace with your coworkers. But even so, you always do fine when you really try. If there is no one in your office who understands this trait, you may feel stressed or misunderstood.

 ELEPHANT: You will stay up all night to complete a task you feel compelled to finish. If you try to work more efficiently, you will find that you have more time. Your relationships with others in the office tend to be rather businesslike.

 SHEEP: You talk too much while working and tend to confuse public and private matters. It's good to enjoy your work, but be careful not to lack seriousness. It is better for you to draw a distinct line between work relationships at the office and those of a more personal nature.

 PEGASUS: The differences between your good moods at work (when you are hardworking) and your bad moods (when you are less productive) are drastic, so the people around you will be completely confused. Very active when you meet with customers or clients, your reputation may differ between your coworkers and those you associate with outside the office.

Party Scene

Take cues from your Charanavi character and learn how you can best interact with others at get togethers.

 WOLF: You tend to eat and drink quietly and at your own pace. Try to be more outgoing and join in the conversation. If you keep trying, you may find yourself laughing and talking with a kindred spirit.

 FAWN: You can tend to stay in one place all night and talk with only a few people. Make an effort to be more sociable and mingle more. Try exchanging contact information with others; you might end up meeting your favorite person at the party.

 MONKEY: At get togethers, you are popular and regarded as a versatile performer. But try to avoid giving the impression that you are only the life of the party. Show your attentiveness to other guests by offering a drink to someone with an empty glass.

 CHEETAH: You are often attracted to the opposite sex and tend to focus your energy on one person very quickly. It can be obvious to others that you are fascinated by him/her, but you don't mind and often make an aggressive approach.

 BLACK PANTHER: You like to run the show at a party, and your attentiveness and caring attitude is nice and impressive to others. You are quite indispensable at get togethers.

 LION: You tend to like attractive, outgoing people, but be considerate of the modest types as well. You are always well dressed, and you can make an even better impression with some tasteful cologne or perfume.

TIGER: When you are under the influence of alcohol, you tend to make blistering remarks to others. Try to avoid lecturing those you don't know well. You will make a better impression if you can show your kindness by offering to replenish others' food and drink.

 TANUKI: You are very considerate of others, and your modest attitude gives a nice impression. But being overly modest can make you seem like a wallflower, so try to make an impressive self-introduction that will have a lasting effect.

 KOALA: In conversation, you tend to bring up sexual topics. Since this can be considered taboo in certain company, be sure to read the atmosphere when deciding what to talk about. Your gentle, smiling face is very attractive to others. Being a good listener is a wise way to make a good impression.

 ELEPHANT: Your feelings tend to run high when you are intoxicated. Don't drink too quickly or force others to. If you meet someone you really like at a party, instead of coming on too strong in the moment, try to be more subtle and follow up with an email or phone call afterward.

 SHEEP: You tend to talk with the same person from beginning to end. Since you're at a party, take the opportunity to meet new people. Move around and mingle more.

 PEGASUS: If you are not in good spirits, you tend to leave a gathering early. But since you are a very attractive person, you can and should be the life of the party. Get decked out in your favorite outfit.

MALE & FEMALE COMPATIBILITY CHART

For the Animal Character Names see pages 12–13.

MALE CHARANAVI CHARACTER NUMBERS 1–15

FEMALE CHARANAVI CHARACTER NUMBERS 1–30

♡	1	2	3	4	5	6	7	8	9	10	11	12	13	14	15
1	52	80	47	13	67	93	20	8	88	75	73	57	35	40	43
2	92	42	40	60	28	85	1	17	35	80	13	50	78	23	37
3	40	20	37	47	72	5	38	97	13	42	62	78	83	55	33
4	15	62	53	42	5	78	75	58	95	37	23	87	13	72	52
5	55	30	87	7	18	75	52	27	82	100	35	23	68	47	83
6	95	32	7	78	72	37	25	28	12	83	98	20	47	55	5
7	17	1	48	75	62	23	15	90	42	68	88	95	35	5	45
8	7	18	97	70	30	47	92	42	35	63	15	55	1	17	38
9	88	23	18	95	73	12	42	20	40	90	63	7	83	97	17
10	75	83	50	37	100	90	73	58	48	18	3	43	67	87	95
11	57	22	68	37	25	98	85	20	65	3	42	77	48	15	67
12	48	63	72	88	38	17	95	62	8	43	77	22	85	58	68
13	22	65	82	13	90	43	18	1	75	57	30	27	38	72	78
14	85	27	58	80	43	88	3	18	97	75	10	52	73	38	55
15	42	22	40	47	68	5	83	18	13	95	62	75	82	53	37
16	98	58	48	37	5	77	72	90	43	18	100	83	13	68	45
17	55	95	63	5	10	77	53	50	60	88	20	98	90	33	62
18	55	70	1	42	37	27	52	67	13	87	82	47	93	65	7
19	27	7	88	97	50	47	10	67	77	60	80	35	22	1	87
20	3	18	60	83	95	63	88	30	55	78	10	52	8	22	97
21	92	82	12	33	73	100	67	78	23	88	62	7	55	50	10
22	68	75	25	38	90	83	98	73	22	13	7	63	58	50	23
23	25	12	53	78	43	58	87	93	50	8	28	48	73	17	52
24	90	70	92	65	53	43	22	67	1	63	38	12	42	78	83
25	27	67	83	15	90	52	17	8	77	97	40	35	48	73	80
26	100	28	55	75	43	87	3	27	52	92	93	48	68	40	53
27	62	98	25	33	68	3	92	73	10	28	58	100	53	48	22
28	15	80	93	38	7	27	73	78	22	32	67	70	98	57	25
29	88	40	13	1	58	72	27	37	68	23	35	65	83	93	12
30	20	68	8	63	97	47	85	65	15	82	33	27	42	77	1

Check your romance compatibility with a mate!

Example: Male #21 / Female #6 = 100% (*A Perfect Match!*)

MALE CHARANAVI CHARACTER NUMBERS 16–30

♡	16	17	18	19	20	21	22	23	24	25	26	27	28	29	30
1	98	72	53	30	3	92	83	42	33	32	100	82	15	37	28
2	57	95	48	72	15	67	65	10	77	75	22	98	63	20	70
3	45	58	1	90	48	12	28	57	92	82	52	27	93	50	8
4	38	3	45	97	67	28	17	73	65	12	68	27	25	1	63
5	5	12	20	62	95	73	72	48	67	65	43	70	8	15	97
6	77	63	17	87	48	100	85	57	45	43	52	3	22	50	40
7	72	67	52	28	85	83	98	87	33	32	3	92	82	37	27
8	67	50	53	87	22	77	75	93	85	8	25	73	72	23	82
9	45	60	13	80	50	37	35	57	1	82	53	33	32	52	15
10	20	23	40	62	68	30	10	8	65	97	70	28	27	82	60
11	100	40	73	83	13	62	5	32	47	45	95	60	58	28	43
12	87	98	20	27	52	7	50	60	12	83	55	100	90	53	25
13	12	83	95	17	8	55	53	73	37	35	68	52	98	85	32
14	77	25	48	1	20	35	33	15	72	70	37	32	30	93	67
15	45	58	8	77	97	12	33	55	80	78	50	32	30	48	1
16	33	3	40	62	63	93	27	87	92	12	65	25	23	8	60
17	3	18	68	45	28	58	100	35	48	83	30	57	7	13	43
18	40	78	43	92	58	12	88	98	22	20	62	5	57	60	17
19	62	37	33	18	72	58	57	85	93	20	8	55	53	73	40
20	82	27	50	87	40	38	37	13	77	1	20	35	33	42	73
21	95	58	20	53	45	40	38	52	5	85	97	15	37	47	18
22	35	100	82	52	47	43	18	5	57	55	48	93	42	78	80
23	85	27	98	83	13	35	3	40	72	70	15	33	100	37	67
24	87	35	17	93	73	5	62	80	20	40	75	60	58	98	18
25	13	38	32	42	1	60	58	75	47	45	87	57	12	70	93
26	72	25	47	8	35	97	33	13	67	65	38	32	30	37	62
27	32	57	8	78	42	15	93	50	82	52	45	37	35	43	7
28	35	5	68	60	52	43	18	100	62	12	53	42	40	3	58
29	8	32	62	80	45	43	90	52	98	22	48	10	3	47	78
30	62	30	23	37	72	12	60	78	40	93	75	5	58	73	35

CONTINUED ON NEXT PAGE >

MALE & FEMALE COMPATIBILITY CHART

MALE CHARANAVI CHARACTER NUMBERS 31–45

♡	31	32	33	34	35	36	37	38	39	40	41	42	43	44	45
1	22	7	87	45	38	95	55	70	77	10	90	50	18	5	85
2	7	18	62	38	8	73	100	47	55	33	43	90	5	30	58
3	88	60	17	35	53	80	77	98	43	30	22	3	87	73	15
4	47	22	43	18	70	85	10	20	93	48	8	77	83	88	40
5	25	33	60	85	45	63	22	32	57	1	10	53	80	42	58
6	93	65	15	92	53	42	18	62	8	60	97	27	82	73	13
7	20	100	77	47	38	30	18	8	70	40	80	93	13	63	73
8	90	52	98	40	10	83	5	20	65	33	43	80	100	32	68
9	78	62	48	93	55	8	77	58	43	38	25	10	67	98	47
10	45	25	38	15	1	63	42	22	35	47	85	88	80	55	93
11	88	18	38	7	30	97	75	17	33	63	52	55	92	12	35
12	47	75	5	70	57	10	93	73	45	92	65	23	32	40	3
13	28	3	62	80	70	33	25	100	58	15	67	20	48	7	60
14	5	17	82	57	13	68	50	23	98	53	28	83	8	45	78
15	92	60	17	38	52	85	73	57	43	93	23	3	90	70	15
16	97	88	38	47	67	85	10	22	32	42	1	73	82	55	35
17	72	93	40	92	32	47	70	42	37	8	15	97	82	27	38
18	48	80	100	90	63	18	45	77	3	73	72	53	95	38	10
19	12	38	65	98	83	42	17	3	82	75	70	25	15	100	63
20	90	28	85	58	93	75	5	17	80	53	32	25	92	47	98
21	65	60	35	25	48	1	63	57	13	22	83	68	30	75	32
22	65	62	40	12	3	53	97	60	33	17	77	87	32	72	37
23	88	10	80	7	38	68	47	95	75	82	32	23	92	22	77
24	32	37	8	85	77	13	30	33	100	88	72	23	48	55	7
25	18	3	63	82	72	43	33	37	62	98	68	25	22	7	85
26	1	17	77	83	12	63	80	23	70	50	95	78	7	20	73
27	88	97	13	23	47	80	60	55	30	18	77	1	87	70	12
28	72	65	95	17	55	82	13	63	33	20	8	75	97	92	37
29	67	33	87	100	50	82	63	30	17	5	42	28	75	95	85
30	88	32	13	83	98	38	25	28	7	80	70	18	90	55	100

FEMALE CHARANAVI CHARACTER NUMBERS 1–30

Example: Male #59 / Female #4 = 100% (*A Perfect Match!*)

MALE CHARANAVI CHARACTER NUMBERS 46–60

♡	46	47	48	49	50	51	52	53	54	55	56	57	58	59	60
1	97	78	48	25	63	62	12	68	27	17	1	60	58	65	23
2	82	93	68	83	25	53	52	32	87	3	27	97	88	12	45
3	32	18	100	63	67	25	23	75	7	65	70	10	95	68	85
4	50	60	90	98	55	35	33	7	82	80	57	32	30	100	92
5	88	28	50	92	93	38	3	13	78	77	40	37	90	17	98
6	90	30	23	35	67	1	58	75	38	80	70	10	88	68	33
7	43	78	50	10	7	57	97	65	25	12	60	55	53	58	22
8	37	13	78	3	27	62	60	95	48	88	28	58	57	12	45
9	87	22	3	92	68	30	28	75	100	65	72	27	85	70	5
10	13	7	72	78	52	33	17	57	92	98	53	32	12	5	77
11	1	50	53	80	10	72	87	27	82	90	93	70	8	23	78
12	67	97	15	28	33	82	80	42	18	30	37	1	78	35	13
13	77	63	93	42	88	23	10	92	47	45	5	87	97	50	40
14	87	12	22	100	40	65	63	47	90	7	42	62	92	95	60
15	35	20	87	63	98	28	27	72	7	88	67	10	25	65	100
16	20	57	70	15	50	95	30	7	80	78	53	28	17	52	75
17	85	22	52	75	23	67	1	12	80	78	25	65	87	17	73
18	75	68	50	25	32	8	85	97	30	28	35	15	83	33	23
19	78	68	23	45	5	90	32	52	95	13	48	30	28	92	43
20	57	12	23	7	43	72	70	48	65	100	45	68	67	15	62
21	93	80	8	87	70	17	43	77	28	27	98	42	90	72	3
22	10	1	67	28	88	45	20	92	85	30	70	95	15	8	27
23	5	30	97	57	18	65	63	45	60	90	20	62	1	42	55
24	82	68	10	95	50	28	27	57	47	45	52	3	25	97	15
25	78	65	23	50	100	30	10	92	53	20	5	88	28	55	95
26	82	10	22	85	42	98	60	45	88	5	18	58	90	15	57
27	20	75	90	27	63	40	95	72	5	85	67	17	38	65	83
28	23	83	87	10	77	50	48	1	30	28	90	47	45	88	85
29	92	38	25	18	53	15	7	60	97	73	57	77	20	55	70
30	92	67	17	45	50	3	22	57	48	95	53	10	87	52	43

CONTINUED ON NEXT PAGE >

MALE & FEMALE COMPATIBILITY CHART

MALE CHARANAVI CHARACTER NUMBERS 1–15

FEMALE CHARANAVI CHARACTER NUMBERS 31–60

♥	1	2	3	4	5	6	7	8	9	10	11	12	13	14	15
31	22	7	68	43	33	95	15	87	65	38	92	50	27	5	88
32	7	22	70	42	27	80	100	52	63	35	15	77	5	18	67
33	90	57	17	35	50	77	73	98	42	87	23	3	62	70	15
34	40	85	33	45	82	55	37	18	93	15	8	70	80	90	30
35	27	15	57	92	45	60	83	13	53	1	30	52	72	18	55
36	93	68	92	63	50	23	27	65	8	60	97	12	40	77	83
37	55	100	72	12	78	37	22	8	83	43	73	93	32	87	68
38	82	48	98	38	25	90	5	20	62	78	13	75	100	32	63
39	80	62	48	93	55	8	78	58	17	35	23	88	67	98	47
40	10	23	43	52	1	67	45	20	38	18	65	92	15	58	93
41	90	42	38	7	12	97	73	40	33	88	23	55	82	27	35
42	50	80	5	77	65	20	93	78	10	90	73	53	33	42	3
43	75	3	82	72	60	30	12	100	50	65	92	18	40	7	80
44	5	30	85	90	45	75	55	28	98	58	12	27	8	52	82
45	90	58	17	38	50	73	72	55	45	93	27	3	82	68	15
46	97	82	32	43	90	58	35	18	28	15	1	70	80	85	30
47	75	93	37	88	30	45	73	20	33	8	53	97	83	13	35
48	47	82	100	88	63	17	45	78	3	73	72	15	95	37	42
49	35	88	65	98	72	42	18	3	82	75	67	27	50	100	63
50	53	25	85	60	93	77	5	23	82	55	12	22	88	48	98
51	68	62	32	22	47	1	67	58	13	18	88	72	25	80	28
52	15	65	40	27	3	58	97	87	35	17	92	72	12	77	37
53	50	28	82	7	13	70	47	95	77	85	32	23	90	45	80
54	30	35	8	88	80	40	27	32	100	85	75	20	53	60	7
55	17	3	82	73	65	37	12	87	55	98	92	25	45	7	80
56	1	25	82	85	38	70	83	23	75	52	95	22	7	47	78
57	70	97	13	32	53	20	68	63	38	27	87	1	90	80	12
58	70	88	95	23	52	58	67	63	35	10	8	75	97	90	37
59	53	12	80	100	42	73	83	10	77	5	33	27	65	95	78
60	28	33	60	92	98	38	27	30	7	77	67	10	90	50	10

Example: Male #18 / Female #33 = 100% (*A Perfect Match!*)

MALE CHARANAVI CHARACTER NUMBERS 16–30

♡	16	17	18	19	20	21	22	23	24	25	26	27	28	29	30
31	97	70	47	10	85	58	57	80	25	17	1	83	55	60	23
32	38	93	75	83	32	62	60	13	50	3	17	97	58	33	47
33	32	20	100	60	63	27	25	72	7	85	67	10	95	65	18
34	42	50	67	98	48	28	12	7	78	77	88	27	25	100	73
35	90	28	48	82	93	37	3	42	70	68	17	35	78	38	98
36	62	33	18	37	70	1	58	78	13	38	73	57	55	72	20
37	10	90	50	25	7	58	97	62	30	28	85	57	13	82	23
38	35	42	72	3	17	58	57	95	47	45	30	55	53	28	80
39	38	20	3	92	68	10	28	75	100	65	72	27	25	70	5
40	50	7	73	78	55	35	33	60	80	98	57	32	30	5	77
41	1	15	53	78	25	70	68	18	80	92	93	67	8	10	77
42	75	97	52	87	35	15	92	43	32	30	38	1	83	37	27
43	68	55	93	15	85	22	20	88	38	37	5	83	97	42	33
44	88	35	25	100	50	72	70	15	67	7	20	68	92	95	63
45	35	23	18	62	98	30	83	70	7	88	65	10	28	63	100
46	40	52	67	73	47	95	12	7	78	77	83	25	23	48	72
47	87	52	55	92	10	70	1	27	82	80	12	68	90	23	77
48	77	68	48	28	30	8	85	97	13	87	33	92	90	32	27
49	15	83	23	45	5	87	30	55	95	48	80	28	10	52	43
50	58	30	20	7	43	72	90	15	67	100	47	70	68	45	63
51	93	85	8	90	75	17	42	82	92	23	98	40	38	77	3
52	23	1	70	32	82	48	47	88	85	10	75	95	45	8	30
53	5	12	97	58	42	65	92	22	62	88	43	63	1	15	57
54	87	72	17	95	55	10	90	62	52	50	57	3	23	97	47
55	70	60	22	15	100	30	28	88	43	42	5	85	27	47	95
56	55	28	20	87	43	98	67	15	63	5	18	65	88	45	60
57	28	85	23	35	73	47	95	82	5	88	77	17	45	75	18
58	20	82	72	27	78	47	17	1	32	30	87	45	43	80	25
59	88	32	23	90	20	68	7	48	97	63	22	67	92	45	60
60	80	63	17	43	45	3	25	52	15	95	48	88	87	47	42

CONTINUED ON NEXT PAGE >

MALE & FEMALE COMPATIBILITY CHART
MALE CHARANAVI CHARACTER NUMBERS 31–45

FEMALE CHARANAVI CHARACTER NUMBERS 31–60

♡	31	32	33	34	35	36	37	38	39	40	41	42	43	44	45
31	20	90	45	67	78	93	48	8	40	63	62	53	13	35	42
32	88	45	43	68	12	48	1	20	37	85	53	57	92	28	40
33	38	22	37	43	68	5	83	97	13	40	58	75	82	52	33
34	72	52	47	32	5	75	68	92	95	17	87	38	60	65	43
35	85	12	77	7	40	67	50	10	73	100	33	25	88	22	75
36	95	35	7	85	75	22	30	32	90	80	98	17	43	52	5
37	20	1	48	70	60	27	52	88	45	15	65	95	18	5	47
38	7	18	97	65	12	43	73	40	33	60	50	85	1	27	37
39	42	22	15	95	73	90	40	18	37	43	63	7	87	97	13
40	75	63	53	42	100	82	13	62	48	37	3	47	70	90	95
41	57	52	65	37	17	98	83	50	62	3	22	75	48	32	63
42	55	72	13	88	40	28	95	70	8	45	82	48	25	67	12
43	10	90	73	53	87	35	17	1	67	48	27	23	78	62	70
44	17	37	62	83	13	65	3	33	97	23	32	57	22	47	60
45	43	25	40	80	67	5	42	22	13	95	60	20	78	52	37
46	98	53	45	13	5	75	68	50	38	27	100	37	62	65	42
47	58	95	67	5	25	78	57	22	63	85	40	98	50	18	65
48	52	70	1	43	35	12	50	67	75	38	83	22	93	65	7
49	17	7	85	97	53	47	25	92	77	13	90	33	22	1	78
50	3	32	62	92	95	65	87	28	57	80	27	52	8	18	97
51	73	87	12	30	78	100	70	83	20	27	63	7	57	48	10
52	73	90	28	38	83	80	98	78	22	33	7	68	63	55	25
53	25	30	55	87	20	60	83	93	52	8	10	48	75	40	83
54	22	73	15	92	58	48	18	70	1	67	37	28	45	82	13
55	10	90	75	58	78	40	23	8	83	97	35	33	13	67	72
56	100	30	58	80	13	62	3	27	53	73	93	50	92	40	57
57	72	98	33	92	78	3	25	83	10	37	67	100	62	55	30
58	77	83	93	13	7	28	73	92	18	33	85	68	98	53	22
59	82	15	58	1	47	62	25	13	55	87	30	52	75	93	57
60	23	65	8	58	97	13	82	62	78	85	35	18	40	73	1

Example: Male #57 / Female #42 = 100% (*A Perfect Match!*)

MALE CHARANAVI CHARACTER NUMBERS 46–60

♡	46	47	48	49	50	51	52	53	54	55	56	57	58	59	60
31	98	82	52	18	3	77	75	37	30	12	100	73	72	32	28
32	65	95	55	8	23	73	87	30	82	90	25	98	72	10	78
33	88	55	1	92	45	12	30	53	80	78	48	28	93	47	8
34	13	3	35	97	62	23	22	83	58	57	63	20	10	1	53
35	5	32	23	58	95	65	80	47	62	87	20	63	8	43	97
36	82	67	10	88	45	100	87	53	25	42	48	3	28	47	15
37	67	63	53	35	40	77	98	80	38	17	3	92	75	42	23
38	87	15	52	83	22	70	68	93	92	8	23	67	88	10	77
39	45	60	77	83	50	33	32	57	1	85	53	12	30	52	82
40	40	22	83	12	72	28	27	8	68	97	88	25	17	87	85
41	100	20	72	85	28	60	5	13	47	45	95	58	87	30	43
42	85	98	47	18	60	7	58	68	23	22	63	100	57	62	17
43	52	25	95	77	8	47	45	63	32	13	58	43	98	57	28
44	80	10	53	1	18	42	87	48	78	77	43	40	38	93	73
45	87	57	8	92	97	12	33	53	77	75	48	32	85	47	1
46	17	3	33	57	88	93	22	92	87	60	63	20	10	8	55
47	3	38	72	43	15	62	100	32	48	47	17	60	7	28	42
48	40	80	20	23	58	57	55	98	18	25	62	5	53	60	10
49	62	37	32	40	68	60	12	73	93	20	8	58	57	70	38
50	83	10	50	75	40	38	37	42	78	1	17	35	33	13	73
51	95	60	65	53	43	37	35	50	5	55	97	15	33	45	52
52	18	100	67	13	50	43	42	5	62	60	53	93	20	52	57
53	78	27	98	68	37	35	3	18	73	72	38	33	100	17	67
54	68	33	25	93	77	5	65	83	43	42	78	12	63	98	38
55	57	77	32	18	1	53	52	68	38	20	63	50	48	62	93
56	77	10	48	8	17	97	35	42	72	90	37	33	32	12	68
57	40	65	8	58	48	15	93	57	22	60	52	43	42	50	7
58	12	5	65	57	48	42	40	100	62	60	50	38	15	3	55
59	8	28	50	72	17	38	37	43	98	85	18	35	3	40	70
60	57	32	12	37	68	55	83	75	22	93	72	5	53	70	20

My Charanavi Companions

*Keep track of birthdays and Charanavi characters
for your friends, family and coworkers here.*

Name: _____ Birthday: ____ / ____ / ____

Character Name / # : _____

Name: _____ Birthday: ____ / ____ / ____

Character Name / # : _____

Name: _____ Birthday: ____ / ____ / ____

Character Name / # : _____

Name: _____ Birthday: ____ / ____ / ____

Character Name / # : _____

Name: _____ Birthday: ____ / ____ / ____

Character Name / # : _____

Name: _____ Birthday: ____ / ____ / ____

Character Name / # : _____

Name: _____ Birthday: ____ / ____ / ____

Character Name / # : _____

Name: _____ Birthday: ____ / ____ / ____

Character Name / # : _____

Name: _____ Birthday: ____ / ____ / ____

Character Name / # : _____

Name: _____ Birthday: ____ / ____ / ____

Character Name / # : _____

Name: _____ Birthday: _____ / _____ / _____

Character Name / # : _____

Name: _____ Birthday: _____ / _____ / _____

Character Name / # : _____

Name: _____ Birthday: _____ / _____ / _____

Character Name / # : _____

Name: _____ Birthday: _____ / _____ / _____

Character Name / # : _____

Name: _____ Birthday: _____ / _____ / _____

Character Name / # : _____

Name: _____ Birthday: _____ / _____ / _____

Character Name / # : _____

Name: _____ Birthday: _____ / _____ / _____

Character Name / # : _____

Name: _____ Birthday: _____ / _____ / _____

Character Name / # : _____

Name: _____ Birthday: _____ / _____ / _____

Character Name / # : _____

Name: _____ Birthday: _____ / _____ / _____

Character Name / # : _____

Name: _____ Birthday: _____ / _____ / _____

Character Name / # : _____

Name: _____ Birthday: _____ / _____ / _____

Character Name / # : _____

*Name:*_____ *Birthday:* ____ / ____ / ____

*Character Name / # :*_____

*Name:*_____ *Birthday:* ____ / ____ / ____

*Character Name / # :*_____

*Name:*_____ *Birthday:* ____ / ____ / ____

*Character Name / # :*_____

*Name:*_____ *Birthday:* ____ / ____ / ____

*Character Name / # :*_____

*Name:*_____ *Birthday:* ____ / ____ / ____

*Character Name / # :*_____

*Name:*_____ *Birthday:* ____ / ____ / ____

*Character Name / # :*_____

*Name:*_____ *Birthday:* ____ / ____ / ____

*Character Name / # :*_____

*Name:*_____ *Birthday:* ____ / ____ / ____

*Character Name / # :*_____

*Name:*_____ *Birthday:* ____ / ____ / ____

*Character Name / # :*_____

*Name:*_____ *Birthday:* ____ / ____ / ____

*Character Name / # :*_____

Index

A, B, C

Active KOALA 126
Adaptable WOLF 32
Adventurous SHEEP. 152
Affectionate TIGER 96
Ambitious MONKEY. 50
Beautiful FAWN 44
Calm PEGASUS 158
Captain LION 88
Caring BLACK PANTHER . . . 72
Cheerful WOLF 24
Chief ELEPHANT 138
Confident TIGER 100
Creative WOLF 28

D, E, F

Delicate ELEPHANT 136
Devoted MONKEY 56
Dignified MONKEY 52
Dramatic PEGASUS 162
Elegant PEGASUS. 164
Emotional LION. 90
Energetic TIGER 98
Flexible PEGASUS 160
Freedom-Loving BLACK
    PANTHER 82
Friendly BLACK PANTHER . . 80

G, H, I

Gentle WOLF. 30
Glorious TANUKI 112
Graceful CHEETAH 68
Harmonious SHEEP 146
Helpful KOALA 130
Honest FAWN 38
Humane SHEEP 150
Independent LION. 86
Innocent SHEEP. 148

J, K, L

King KOALA 124
Liberty TIGER 106
Lovable WOLF. 34

M, N, O

Marathon CHEETAH. 62
Merciful KOALA 122
Mighty-Hearted TANUKI . . 116
Optimistic TIGER. 102

P, Q, R

Passionate BLACK
    PANTHER 74
Playful MONKEY 54
Popular ELEPHANT 134
Potential TANUKI. 114
Powerful TIGER. 104
Protective MONKEY. 58
Reliable SHEEP 154
Restless MONKEY 48
Romantic KOALA 128
Rushing ELEPHANT 140

S, T, U, V

Sensitive LION 92
Sentimental BLACK
    PANTHER 76
Sociable TANUKI 110
Solitary SHEEP. 144
Soulful BLACK PANTHER . . . 78
Sprinting CHEETAH 64
Steady FAWN 42
Strong-Willed FAWN. 40
Swift KOALA. 120
Tough CHEETAH 66

W, X, Y, Z

Wandering WOLF. 26

The Author: Masahiro Tsurumoto

(Glorious Tanuki) was born in Tokyo on April 29, 1957. He holds a degree in law from Gakushuin University.

After working for Meiji Life Insurance Company, he established the Institute of Koseishinrigaku in 1997 and took office as the director. That same year, he established @NOA, Inc., and became the company's representative director. In 2000, Tsurumoto established Charanavi.com, Inc., and since then has served as representative director.

He has published thirty books, including *Koseishinrigaku (Charanavi)*, *Charanavi for Business*, *Animal Charanavi*, *Understanding the Character and Compatibility with Animal Charanavi*, *Love Charanavi* and *Charanavi for Parents* among others.

Tsurumoto presents to companies, hospitals and schools throughout Japan, Los Angeles, San Francisco and Las Vegas.

The Translator: Chikako Saito *(Reliable Sheep)*

was born in 1952. She spent four years of her childhood (1961–1965) in Washington, D.C., and graduated from University of the Sacred Heart, Tokyo, with a degree in Human Relations.

She has been a certified Charanavi lecturer/counselor since 2004 and was chosen by the author, Mr. Tsurumoto, as translator of this book. Through her work, she wishes to make people happier.

Charanavi Head Office in Japan

Koseishinrigaku Kenkyujo
1-4-4 9F, Shiba Daimon
Minatoku, Tokyo,
105-0012, Japan

Phone: (81) 3-5405-9421
Fax: (81) 3-5405-9420

www.charanavi.com
www.noa-group.co.jp
Email: info@noa-group.co.jp

Charanavi USA

Now you can find out your Charanavi character online!

www.charanaviusa.com

Discover your character today by entering your birthday at the above website.